THE MUNCHKIN® BOOK

READ THE ESSAYS
(AB)USE THE RULES * WIN THE GAME

EDITED BY JAMES LOWDER

GAME RULES BY STEVE JACKSON AND ANDREW HACKARD

RULES ASSISTANCE BY DEVIN LEWIS

ARTWORK BY JOHN KOVALIC

 An Imprint of
BenBella Books, Inc.
Dallas, Texas

10300 North Central Expressway, Suite 530
Dallas, TX 75231
www.benbellabooks.com
www.smartpopbooks.com
Send feedback to feedback@benbellabooks.com

Printed in the United States of America
10 9 8 7 6 5 4 3 2 1

Library of Congress Cataloging-in-Publication Data is available for this title.
978-1-939529-15-2

Executive Editor, Steve Jackson Games: Miranda Horner
Copyediting by James Fraleigh
Proofreading by Brittney Martinez and Sarah Vostok
Text design and composition by Publishers' Design and Production Services, Inc.
Front cover by Kit Sweeney
Full cover by Sarah Dombrowsky
Printed by Lake Book Manufacturing

Distributed by Perseus Distribution
www.perseusdistribution.com

To place orders through Perseus Distribution:
Tel: 800-343-4499
Fax: 800-351-5073
E-mail: orderentry@perseusbooks.com

Significant discounts for bulk sales are available. Please contact Aida Herrera at aida@benbellabooks.com.

CONTENTS

THROW THE BOOK AT 'EM

To use the rules in this book, the book must be present in the vicinity of the table. Only one rule may be used in a game of *Munchkin*, and only one per day (excessive use will very likely see the book abused in ways the owner will regret and/or need stitches for). The rule to be used must be chosen before the game starts. Some will take effect immediately; some can be saved until the most advantageous and munchkinly moment.

SILLIEST IS BEST

You may play one Class or Race or Accent or Birthright or Faction or Loyalty or Mojo that is not present in the set or sets you are currently playing with. It cannot be lost to Bad Stuff or to Death.

FOREWORD
WHY I LOVE TO DANCE IN PANTS MACABRE

Ed Greenwood

In the game of life, some of us are gamers.

Yes, those people in jeans and T-shirts – or, ahem, costumes – who sit around playing games.

We love our roleplaying games. And some of us *really* love games that parody them, that let us laugh at ourselves. Laugh at those *other* gamers, I mean – the immature, play-to-win "munchkin" sorts, not us, oh no, nothing to see here, ma'am, please just move along . . . no, a little farther, thankyouverymuch.

Anyway, this flood of love brings many of us inevitably to *Munchkin*.

A parody game. That can also be played as one of the most competitive card games going. (Move over, Crazy Eights, and put away those shinguards, bridge players.) A game that inspires ardent devotion and the purchase of a seemingly endless number of expansion sets that just add to the fun, not to mention the standalone *Munchkin* variants that skewer other genres, to say nothing of the *Munchkin* boardgame and, of course, T-shirts and shot glasses and –

Why, yes, I did just say "shot glasses."

We love the game enough not just to argue over the rules – *all* gamers argue over almost every rule in nigh every sort of game, including, my police officer friends tell me, the so-called rules of life – but also to have the rules major-league revamped in the Great 2010 Changeover. (Which included "fixing" a too-powerful card called, our fellow munchkins help us – and, yes, that was a *Munchkin*-subtle joke, there – "Kneepads of Allure.") We love the game enough to talk about it for hours on end.

In fact, let me tell you about the time my –

All right, I can see your eyes glazing over. That tells me you're a gamer. Non-gamers haven't learned how deadly what follows those words can be unless they're married to a gamer, or best friends with one. Then they know what that lead-in promises, but also just how dreadfully important such stories are to the gamer telling them. They also have a coping strategy: You Had To Be There, yes, but just keep smiling and nodding and saying "Uh huh" and asking breathlessly, "So what did you do *then* . . . ?" Eventually the earnest teller will run down and you can flee. (*Always* have an escape route planned in life, whether you need to sneak out of a mind-numbing office cubicle so you can feel fresh air on your face, or so you can spend quality time with the pet African elephant you're not supposed to have, or so you can avoid the boss when he comes looking for a scapegoat with *that* look in his eyes.)

Anyway, let me tell you my "about the time my" story because – I promise! – it's not about my four-armed, two-headed, prehensile-tailed drow paladin with her twin ninja star-firing rapiers and pneumatic show armor, which has chase lights around the breastworks and self-oiling hips. Not this time. No, it's about why *Munchkin* matters to *me*. And should, to you.

When we're young, if we're lucky, there's time for *fun* in life. Time to play, time to daydream, time to dawdle, time to get muddy, to discover books . . . time for ourselves. As the years move along, rules creep in, and obligations, and the need to make bucks – and it all takes so much time. All those demands gobble up a lot of the hours in which we used to have fun. Worries proliferate, stakes become higher, stress and tension visit us a lot more often or even become constant companions, and life gets grayer. Boo hoo, happens to all of us, I know, and when my father and grandfather were young, they walked the proverbial uphill both ways to school and back, and had to work blahblahblah.

So let me speak of a friend of mine who came back from a war grayer than many. All grim, no smiles, stone-faced. All the fun drained – scorched – right out of him. Didn't want to talk, didn't want to go out and do things, certainly didn't want to play games. Especially games about war. "War's no game," he snarled once, walking out on a roleplaying session that was just about to start.

So, of course, being gamers, we tricked him into a game.

He still knew how to drink, and there came a night and a bar where three guys with many bottles on their table were playing cards. They called him over and invited him to join in. He did, but instead of hearts and spades, the cards in the hand he was dealt had goofy art on them and even goofier names. He went even more stone-faced, snared a beer, and started to fold his hand. Which was when someone played a card that startled him into half-grinning and staying put. Not long after that, he was laughing out loud – and asking what the game was and when we could play it again.

So we gave him the cards and told him tomorrow night, at his place, and we'd bring the beer. He laughed again as he said, "Great!"

I don't know if he's played any other sorts of games since then, but he plays *Munchkin* whenever he can. And the stone face is gone. He's not the type to use the word *love*, but I know he loves *Munchkin*.

And why not? You've got to love a game that has expansion sets entitled *Beating a Dead Horse* and *Jump the Shark.* Not to mention *Cheat With Both Hands.* And has cards called "Really Secret Agent" and "Rat on a Stick" and "Foof Gun." (Not to mention monster enhancement cards called ". . . With Bagpipes" and ". . . With Extra Cheese" and "Better Costume Than Yours.") Or a card that really is labeled "You'll Take Away My Toy When You Pry It From My Cold, Dead Hands."

I personally love watching the faces of highbrow non-gamer friends who are busily sneering at "this silly game" when cards entitled "Mephitic," "Rugose," and "Squamous" come up in play. Not to mention "Tumescent." (No, kids, don't play *Munchkin* in class. Cards with names like that get a game confiscated faster than you can draw breath. And for good. Teachers like to play games, too. And win.)

You've got to love a game – or at least I do – that allows characters to wear Three Years of Dirt and yet still have a character class of Playboy.

You've got to love a game that has a monster called the Floating Nose. And another called the Tongue Demon. Not to mention James Bomb, or Squidzilla, or the Worminator, or the Plutonium Dragon. And, of course, the legendary, make-the-most-valiant-hero-quake-in-terror Gazebo!

And I, specifically, love the glee I feel when the Chicken on Your Head curse enters play. Except when it lands on *my* character's head, of course. . . .

Yes, this is a supremely silly game that *works.* Along the way it celebrates not just gamer culture, but the larger culture that enwraps almost everyone alive in the Western world, no matter how they try to avoid, shun, or renounce it – often while secretly enjoying aspects of it as guilty pleasures.

Munchkin is a pleasure, all right. And it's certainly "guilty," in that all gamers are guilty of contributing to the things Steve Jackson reacted to, lampooned, and slyly included in this classic of a game.

If you love the game already, turn the page and waste not another second reading my ramblings.

If this is your introduction to *Munchkin*, turn the page and get on with it. Don't worry. You'll pick up the rules as you go along; it really is easy.

And if you're just getting settled into *Munchkin*, you've come to the right place. Sit down, pick up your hand of goofy cards, and start laughing. ✳

Ed Greenwood is an amiable, bearded Canadian writer, game designer, and librarian best known as the creator of the Forgotten Realms fantasy world. He sold his first fiction at age six, and over the almost five decades since, has published more than 200 books that have sold millions of copies worldwide in over two dozen languages. Ed writes fantasy, SF, horror, steampunk, and pulp adventure, in prose and in comic books, and has won several dozen writing and gaming awards, including multiple Origins Awards and ENnies. He was elected to the Academy of Adventure Gaming Arts and Design Hall of Fame in 2003. He has judged the World Fantasy Awards and the Sunburst Awards, hosted radio shows, acted onstage, explored caves, jousted, and been Santa Claus (but not all on the same day). Ed shares an old Ontario farmhouse with his wife and the head of the household, a small but imperious cat. This ramshackle mansion sags under the weight of more than 80,000 books. Ed's most recent novels include *The Iron Assassin*, a steampunk romp from Tor Books; *Spellstorm*, a Forgotten Realms book from Wizards of the Coast; and *Hellmaw: Your World Is Doomed!*, the first release from The Ed Greenwood Group.

DIFFERENT PERSPECTIVE

You gain a +5 to combat as long as all the cards you have in play are upside down or sideways relative to you.

INTRODUCTION
THE SPACE BETWEEN THE CARDS

James Lowder

I t was Dave Arneson who got me to play *Munchkin* for the first time. As the gaming history aficionados among you may already know, Dave co-created *Dungeons & Dragons*. He was also a nice guy who loved games – not just designing them, but playing them and sharing his enthusiasm for them. So in 2006, when I was putting together a roster of industry notables I hoped would contribute to an essay anthology about the best hobby games, Dave's name appeared near the top of the list. In fact, the book as I'd envisioned it would have a lot in common with the conversations about games I'd had with Dave the few times our paths crossed at conventions, though probably with fewer jokes about our mutual former employer, TSR.

Dave responded to my invitation by rattling off a few games he'd gladly champion. His selections were characteristically diverse and demonstrated how current he'd been keeping on the hobby. For every classic he mentioned, like M. A. R. Barker's *Empire of the Petal Throne*, he listed several newer designs, such as *Carcassonne* and *HeroClix*. He finally settled on a title less than a year old at the time of our conversation: Dirk Henn's excellent resource management game, *Shogun*.

Sadly, that essay never saw completion. First Dave's teaching schedule, then his failing health precluded him from ever finishing his contribution to *Hobby Games: The 100 Best*, but the book's subject clearly inspired him. Even after he'd settled on his topic, I received several short emails in which he suggested more titles he thought belonged on that list of the 100 best, games he hoped some other essayist would cover. I shared Dave's zeal for most of the designs he mentioned. When the subject of *Munchkin* came up, though, I politely demurred.

"I'll bet you haven't played it much," Dave noted – quite accurately, as it turned out.

Oh, I was aware of *Munchkin* from the moment designer Steve Jackson and artist John Kovalic unleashed it upon the world in 2001. It would have been impossible for me to miss its debut. I was working extensively in the hobby game market at the time, and *Munchkin*'s launch was a noteworthy event in that little corner of the publishing industry. The core set recorded very strong initial sales and, more importantly, inspired a vocal fan base, the beginnings of what would become a veritable crusading army of players eager to spread the word of *Munchkin*'s glories. The core set subsequently went on to capture the Origins Award that year for Best Traditional Card Game, a critical affirmation to go along with all the popular success. So it was pretty clear to everyone paying the least bit of attention that Steve Jackson Games had hit upon something big.

Given the creators involved, I should have been one of *Munchkin*'s early adopters. Steve Jackson's designs hold a prominent place in my gaming history. I got into the hobby in the late 1970s through roleplaying games such as *Dungeons & Dragons* and *Villains and Vigilantes*, and relatively obscure board games such as Eon's *Cosmic Encounter*, but early in my gaming life I also faced annihilation beneath the treads of a gigantic robot tank in Steve's wargame *Ogre*, vied for secret control of the world through his card game *Illuminati*, and blasted my way across the post-apocalyptic future in the classic vehicular combat game *Car Wars*, which Steve designed with Chad Irby. Later, I became a fan of SJ Games' roleplaying system, *GURPS*, and its wonderfully researched supplements, which covered topics as wildly diverse as Imperial Rome and the paranoid cult TV series *The Prisoner*, Miskatonic University and the Scarlet Pimpernel. Shortly before *Munchkin's* release, Steve even hired me to serve as editorial ringmaster for a book of RPG villains dreamed up by *GURPS* fans.

My admiration for artist John Kovalic's work runs just as deep. I've been an avid follower of his comic strip *Dork Tower*, which chronicles the lives and loves of a cadre of gamers in the fictional town of Mud Bay, Wisconsin, since shortly after its debut. In the late 1990s, it started popping up in a few of the hobby-themed magazines for which I occasionally wrote; before I knew it, *Dork Tower* was my first destination when opening up a new issue of *Dragon* or *Shadis*. I've faithfully followed the strip since then, as John transitioned it first to comic book form, then to a webcomic. And there are his stealth projects, like providing the charming apple illustrations for the best-selling game *Apples to Apples*. You can also stumble across John's work outside of gaming in such little-read markets as *The New York Times* and *Rolling Stone*.

So I should have been an easy sell for a fantasy gaming-themed card game by Jackson and Kovalic, right? I wasn't, though.

Looking back, it's difficult for me to pin down exactly what stopped me from picking up *Munchkin* at my local hobby shop. I sometimes find screw-your-neighbor designs frustrating. I also recall feeling a bit overwhelmed by the number of supplements and new base sets that followed hard on the heels of the core game's release; it's always a challenge to sort out which add-ons are necessary to fully enjoy a game once a series really begins to take off. There was *Munchkin's* theme, too. I spent the first few years of my publishing career working on, among other things, the Forgotten Realms, a setting often criticized by narrative-focused hobbyists as a haven for power-gaming munchkins. I couldn't imagine a way to make the generally painful "right way to play an RPG" debate entertaining, even as a spoof.

The art was the first thing that struck me when, prompted by Dave Arneson's insightful observation, I finally bought and unboxed

Munchkin. John's drawings were charming, as expected, and packed with knowing nods to gaming culture. (Essays in this collection reference the story behind the "Gazebo" monster card, for example.) The illustrations were also narratively evocative, to borrow a phrase from academia. That means there's a story implied in such cards as "Pretty Balloons," "Sleep Potion," and "Out to Lunch," events that led to the moments of conflict they capture – or the inevitably bad consequences of those frozen actions. The curse cards are especially rich in suggested story. I don't know about you, but I'd like to hear the tale that resulted in that chicken perching on the head of the justifiably annoyed Thief, or the sequel, where he freed himself from the poultry pompadour.

As I looked a little deeper, Steve's text did its part to keep the mood light, even while fleshing out the game's setting. Professional courtesy, we learn, prevents Lawyers from attacking a Thief, though they're more than happy to slap anyone else with an injunction that allows all the other munchkins at the table to rob them of a card. Many times the text cuts right to the point, but in a way that begged for a more detailed explanation. "You should know better than to pick up a duck in a dungeon," munchkins and their minders are admonished when the "Duck of Doom" curse card comes into play. As with the head-sitting chicken, players surely wonder about the ducks that apparently roam the *Munchkin* dungeons in great numbers, punishing anyone who foolishly handles them.

As for the game itself, conflict is central to *Munchkin*, to be certain, but the text and the art both frame that conflict in such a funny, friendly way that players must laugh their way through it. As I noted earlier, I'm not a huge fan of screw-your-neighbor designs. My wife is downright opposed to them. (Kind person that she is, she would have more fun with the tile-laying game *Carcassonne* if it were an exercise in cooperative map-building, not a contest where players occasionally direct a river into the courtyard of a rival's unfinished keep.) Yet she and I and our teenaged son can all agree on *Munchkin* when family night rolls around, and we play it with only good-natured clashes.

That's an impressive feat *Munchkin* pulls off there.

The secret is in the design. Each new base set takes a genre and captures its essence. Steve and John and *Munchkin* czar Andrew Hackard toss all of the genre's notable examples into the hopper and distill them down to a set of tropes and trappings that can be rendered in miniature, on 3⅜" by 2¼" cards. On their own, the cards can be delightful and amusing, but their real power becomes apparent during play.  They shape the story being told around the gaming table by providing touchstones that cheerfully remind the players of the genre's greatest hits. The cards identify the central and smile-worthy elements of a zombie yarn or fantasy dungeon crawl or martial arts epic, depending upon what flavor of *Munchkin* you've selected.

It's the players who connect those fragments. Their laughter and their frantic negotiations and, yes, even their conflict fill the spaces between the cards. Their play sweeps up all the disparate tropes and characters and bits of setting and gives them life as part of a new unified tale. The exact composition of that tale – the nature of the heroes involved and the way the combat goes down, whether the Tuba of Charm works its magic as intended or a curse strips the munchkin of that fabled instrument at just the wrong time – depends upon the assembled players. Everyone brings a different perspective to the table, after all. Given that and the endless combinations of available cards, no two *Munchkin* sessions are ever going to be exactly the same.

We tried for the same sort of diversity with the essays in this collection. They've been penned by people who know *Munchkin* from the inside, as designers and artists and editors, and by others who adore it as players and enthusiasts. The essays offer glimpses into the process by which *Munchkin* games and associated cool stuff are created, the comedy theory behind its success, even what *Munchkin* can teach us about that old "right way to play an RPG" debate (in ways we hope are both entertaining and enlightening). Some of the material is serious, much of it whimsical. Even if you're a diehard fan, you should gain some new insights into *Munchkin* here, in addition to adding some nifty new rules to your gameplay arsenal.

Hey, it wouldn't really be a *Munchkin* product if it didn't come with playable rules.

That's been a given pretty much from the moment I first discussed this project with the teams at BenBella and Steve Jackson Games. New rules were something everyone wanted to see, and the boffins over at SJ Games did a bang-up job creating them, drawing their inspiration directly from each essay's content. John Kovalic somehow found room in his insanely busy schedule to create original art for the game rules, too. All told, this makes *The Munchkin Book* a part of the game as well as a commentary about the game.

If we got any more meta, the book might vanish into a self-referential paradox and take us all with it.

Instead, we'll invite you to put down that Hammer of Kneecapping and Cheese Grater of Peace, settle back on that whopping great treasure Hoard with a flute of Yuppie Water, and let us share some interesting and amusing things about *Munchkin*. If you were bright enough to get to the party early, we salute your obviously superior judgment. If you're a relative newcomer, great to see you, too. We're happy it didn't take Squidzilla's tentackly grasp (or the understated goading of a game design legend) to get you here.

And if you're paging through this book in the hope it might provide some clue as to why *Munchkin* seems to be popping up everywhere you go, from hobby stores and comic book shops to mega-chain retailers, we're betting that the collective enthusiasm contained within these pages will make you want to give it a try. Don't worry about coming in late. There are always more monsters to kill, more treasure to be stolen, and more buddies to be stabbed – and a whole lot of fun to be had while doing it. ✳

James Lowder has directed lines or series for both large and small publishing houses and has helmed more than a dozen critically acclaimed anthologies, including *Madness on the Orient Express, Curse of the Full Moon,* and the Smart Pop collections *Triumph of The Walking Dead* and *Beyond the Wall.* As a writer, his credits include the best-selling, widely translated dark fantasy novels *Prince of Lies* and *Knight of the Black Rose,* short fiction for such anthologies as *Shadows over Baker Street* and *Genius Loci,* and comic book scripts for Image, DC, and Desperado. He's written hundreds of reviews and essays for publications ranging from *Amazing Stories* and *The New England Journal of History* to BenBella's *King Kong is Back!* and *The Unauthorized X-Men.* His work has received five Origins Awards and an ENnie Award, and been a finalist for the International Horror Guild Award and the Stoker Award. He's just the sort of person who would pick up a duck found wandering a dungeon, consequences be damned.

NUMEROLOGICAL NONSENSE

If you can find numbers on your own cards which can be added, subtracted, multiplied, or divided in any way to give your age in years, go up two levels. (This is obviously easiest for younger players. If your age is 50+, especially if it's prime, too bad.)

MUNCHKIN BY THE NUMBERS

Steve Jackson

Numbers are important! Without numbers, we could only count as high as we have fingers – which is, come to think of it, how many levels it generally takes to win *Munchkin*. And I could make an argument that if it doesn't help you win *Munchkin*, it's not really important after all. Then again, if we couldn't count past 10, any time we fought a monster above level 9 we'd end up in a tie. And, as we all know, Warriors win ties. So Warriors would have an advantage, and the game would be unbalanced. We can't have that, so numbers must be important after all.

So here are a bunch of *Munchkin* numbers for you, starting with:

Month and year I finished this essay: 11/2015. All comments and numbers are accurate as of that date. Since you're reading this later, you can assume that many of the numbers are bigger. At least, I sure hope so!

THE EARLY DAYS

Year in which munchkin *entered geek language as a term for the person who would do anything to "win" an RPG:* 1983, more or less.

The term can be traced to a party game at a Pacificon involving Jeff Okamoto, Sandy Petersen, and others. (Google the phrase "Real Men, Real Roleplayers, Loonies and Munchkins." Go ahead, do it.) This became an Internet meme when the Internet was still pretty much unknown outside labs and universities, and long before the term *meme* came into fashion. A lot of people posted their own ideas of what the Real Men, Real Roleplayers, Loonies, and Munchkins would do in various situations. (I contributed a few myself. . . .)

An example, taken from near the beginning of the file and so quite possibly among the very first ones:

Favorite Attack Style:
> *Real Men* shout their war cry, and wade into battle.
> *Real Roleplayers* parry, counterattack, and protect comrades' backs.
> *Loonies* throw their sword at opponent, then attack with scabbard and lunchbox.
> *Munchkins* leap in with secret "twisted lotus" ninja decapitation strike.

Favorite Way to Die:
> *Real Men* in battle, with boots on, going down swinging.
> *Real Roleplayers* on deathbed, after lengthy dramatic farewell speech.
> *Loonies* laughing while jumping into a portable hole, and carrying a bag of holding.
> *Munchkins* Die? You're kidding, right?

If you want to read more, the Internet is your friend!

Year in which card games took over everybody's brain: 1993.

Thank you, *Magic: The Gathering*. While *MtG* wasn't the first collectible card game, it was arguably the first really good one. It was certainly the first that most people heard of. Many players abandoned boardgames and RPGs in favor of card games around this time.

Years in which the collectible card game fad weakened, taking several game publishers and some distributors with it: 1995–1997, depending on your viewpoint.

Though *Magic* remained strong, and occasional hit CCGs continued to appear, the field as a whole weakened drastically. But non-collectible card games had increased in popularity along with *Magic*, and to this day they're strong . . . and *Munchkin* is helping to keep them that way. That makes me happy.

Year in which I started writing the card game that would become Munchkin: 2000.

I thought that it would be fun to do a parody of bad dungeon crawls. The goal was to write a silly, fast-playing card game about killing monsters and taking their stuff.

Time I have saved so far in this essay by looking up release dates for my own games on Wikipedia *and* BoardGameGeek *rather than walking across the office to the bookshelf:* At least 10 minutes.

In a few generations, we will completely evolve away from the need for feet, and we will grow extra fingers for faster keyboarding, up until voice-to-text is perfected, at which point we will lose the need for all the fingers except one, which we will use to stab the power button when we need to reboot, which will probably be every few days just like it is now. But I digress. . . .

Year in which I first realized Munchkin *would be a hit:* Definitely not 2000.

I had no idea how big this thing would get. No idea at all.

Altitude at which many of the original Munchkin *cards were written:* 35,000 feet, more or less, on a flight from Austin to Phoenix to attend HexaCon 10.

I already had the rules drafted, but I needed a lot more cards! I took a stack of blank cards from *Illuminati: New World Order* on the flight, thought up cards, and wrote them down in blue Sharpie until my hand was tired. Then I dictated to Monica Stephens, who was in the next seat. Her cards looked a lot neater than mine. She also started a playtest tradition that continues to this day: she looked at the card text and tried, creatively and maliciously, to misread it . . . because that's what the players will do!

Date and ZIP code of the first game of Munchkin *ever:* 7/14/2000, 85250.

We used those hand-drawn cards. Monica and I played with a group of the Men In Black (our company demo team), including cell leader Jessie Foster, at HexaCon's hotel in Scottsdale. We had fun. A lot of games don't survive the first playtest. This one came through with flying colors and lots of yelling and giggling.

Number of cards totally nuked in the first playtest: One.

The "Derby of Death Defiance" proved to be a nearly pointless piece of headgear, because all it did was keep you from dying, and dying was no big deal. I suppose we could put it back in with a big bonus, and the "don't die" as a minor side effect. . . .

Stock number: 1408.

The *14* meant small boxed games, and *08* came after *07.* So, no, it was not a "significant" stock number. We had *no idea* that *Munchkin* would turn into our most successful line ever. If we had, it would have gotten a more interesting number, like OMG00001. (Sometimes we really do manage to assign a stock number that means something. *Zombie Dice* is 131313. The Designer's Edition of *Ogre* is 1977, for the year the game was originally released.)

The one significant stock number in the Munchkin *series:* 1503.

That's *Munchkin Apocalypse*. Can you figure out why it's significant?

Retail price of the original game: $24.95.

Fifteen years later, it is still $24.95. The print runs have gotten so big that economies of scale have kept up with inflation. We will eventually have to raise that price, though, so go out and buy six copies now. *Right* now, do you hear me?

Print Statistics

Ship date of the first printing of Munchkin*:* 7/16/2001.

Quantity in the first printing: 5,000.

No, that wasn't nearly enough. So the second printing shipped less than six months later: 12/3/2001. This time we did 10,000, and that wasn't enough, either. So we kept ordering more copies.

Number of printings so far: 29.

That's just the base game of *Munchkin*, and just in English.

Quantity in the largest printing of the basic Munchkin *set:* 130,000.

Last-minute editing note: As this book heads off to print, the 29th printing has arrived and is being shipped, and the 30th printing is on the schedule.

Number of languages Munchkin *has been translated into:* 17, with one more on the way.

Right now, it's available in Chinese (both Simplified and Traditional), Dutch, Finnish, French, German, Greek, Hebrew, Hungarian, Italian, Polish, Portuguese, Russian, Spanish, and Ukrainian. The Japanese and Korean editions are out of print at the moment. Czech is coming. Sadly, we don't have it in Punjabi yet.

New fan group we'd have if we translated it to Punjabi: Six.

Number of different core sets – that is, individually playable Munchkin *games with different themes:* 18 as of this writing, with more on the way.

Total numbers of Munchkin *games in print as of November 2015:*

* 1,162,024 copies of the original game in English.
* 1,384,604 copies of other core sets (*Zombies*, *Booty*, and so on) in English.
* 3,121,439 copies of other *Munchkin* items (supplements, boosters, and so on) in English.
* 106,050 copies of *Munchkin Quest* and supplements in English.
* 1,851,164 *Munchkin* games, supplements, and everything else in languages other than English.
* 7,625,281 total of the above!

ART IS THE NOISE A SEAL MAKES

Number of cards John Kovalic has drawn: Over 5,000.

There was even a special card to commemorate John's prolific pen. (I suppose nowadays, I should say, "his wondrous Wacom.") The "Mystic Correspondence" card was the 2,007th one he drew, and he did it in 2007. Should we do another special one when he hits 10,000?

Number of custom cards I have made for fans at conventions with my own pathetic sketches or no art at all: Hundreds!

At one point, we really overdid this by releasing the promo cards "John Kovalic Draws a Wandering Monster," which gives a bonus if John draws a monster on it, and "Evil Stevie Changes the Rules," which, if I bescribble it with a rule, becomes official. Both of these have been a lot of fun for us, and both have led to serious hand cramps at autograph sessions, so now we control the distribution of those cards very tightly. But if you look at our group on Flickr (we're SteveJacksonGames), there's a photoset for "Evil Stevie Changes the Rules" – 73 photos of cards made over just five days at the Essen game fair in 2008.

As far as I know there is no gallery of the cards John has drawn for fans . . . which is a shame, because original Kovalic cartoons are a lot cuter than original Jackson smears.

Number of different versions of the Munchkin *figure that have appeared on the box cover:* Four, all drawn by John Kovalic.

The original "mean dot-eyes" version was a huge hit, but I was concerned that it might not allow enough scope for animation in a cartoon or computer game. So John created the "pointy eyes" version, which was on the box for a couple of printings. Then, for one printing, there was a sort of transitional version, and then the current "round eyes" character model. The "super deformed" version with the head exaggerated relative to the body was used on a *Munchkin* journal, not a box cover. (Flower, the Girl Munchkin from *Unnatural Axe*, got a makeover recently, too.)

Number of Munchkin *games ever won by John Kovalic:* Exactly one!

He plays a lot, but people always assume that because he draws the cards he must be some sort of Deadly Killer Munchkin, so they always team up on him. So he's still looking for his second victory.

Weight of the Munchkin *mascot costume:* 68 pounds.

Similar to a sports team mascot, this guy, with several different people inside,[1] has been a hit at various conventions. He went to Essen (where he just loved all the LARP weapons for sale) and PAX (where he played *Guitar Hero* like a pro). The costume now belongs to Pegasus, which publishes *Munchkin* in Germany, and there are rumors of a new one being created by another European translator. But wearing this heavy suit and then prancing around like a maniac is a hard, athletic job. So when you see the Munchkin at an event, wave!

PLAYING TO WIN

Number of cards in the Munchkin *database:* 6,218, though this number changes every few weeks.

We keep the database in Filemaker Pro. It has a record for every card we have ever published (as well as a few that we're saving for later). Sets in progress have their own databases, which are merged with the main database after they get to print. Without these databases, we would go completely insane trying to avoid accidental duplication of card names and so on. (Of course, sometimes we duplicate on purpose,[2] which is why if you have both *Star Munchkin* and *Super Munchkin*, you can be a Mutant Mutant.)

Number of doors and treasures in the basic Munchkin *game:* 94 doors, 74 treasures.

This number has varied a bit across different printings. A few years into the game, we found that we could save money by printing

---

[1] Number of people wearing the costume at any one time: One.
[2] Number of different sets in which Great Cthulhu has appeared: Three. So far.

two 84-card sheets and using the same back design for each sheet, which meant that doors and treasures had to be even numbers. Later, it stopped mattering, so the door/treasure mix varies slightly between core sets, depending on how many really stupid ideas we have for each kind of card.

Number of different races, classes, loyalties, mojos, factions, and accents in all versions of the game: 88.

Yes, really.

Number of edible Munchkin *items we have released:* One.

The *Munchkin Resurrection Cookie* (2008) was a real cookie. It not only let you avoid death (which, as I noted, is not a terribly big deal in *Munchkin*) but also let you avoid any level loss or other bad stuff associated with death. Also, it was yummy.

What happened to most of those cookies: 8.

Number of drinkable Munchkin *items we have released:* Also one.

Munchkin Water (2007) was a promo item created for a GAMA Trade Show in Las Vegas. It was a half-liter of perfectly good water, but more important, it gave the drinker a total combat bonus of +3. We had cases and cases of the stuff in the booth and were giving them away like mad . . . until the hotel came down on us and demanded that we stop. It turns out that they sell water for several bucks a bottle, and they don't like anybody cutting in on their action.

Number of extra cards you start with when you wear an official Munchkin *shirt:* One.

The "promo items give you bonuses" gimmick has become integral to the game, at least as it's played by the insane/devoted fans. We've been accused of demonic cleverness in getting you to buy extra stuff. It all started with the original *Munchkin* T-shirt, and the fact is, it was a random whim as the shirt was going to press, as was the meta-gimmick of increasing the bonus if the shirt was signed. But players thought it was funny, so we did it again and again, with more shirts, and bookmarks, and dice, and all kinds of silly stuff. Over the years, John and I have signed a lot of shirts, and Greg Hyland, Andrew Hackard, and Wil Wheaton now have shirt-enhancing powers as well!

Number of promo items that we ended up universally banning from tournament play: One.

The *Official Munchkin Cthulhu Bookmark of Udder Ridiculousness*, which lets the player bring his own Cthulhu Mythos book as a prop, is just too easy to subvert.

Maximum winning level in the game: You think that you win at level 10, right? Well, not always.

The card "Mine Goes to 11!" makes the winning level 11, or 22 in *Epic* games. The "Dungeon of Extra Effort" has similar effects. By the way they are worded, those two cards don't stack, so you can't use them together to make the winning level 12. But there's nothing except our own discretion and good judgment to keep us from issuing a card that simply adds 1 to the current level required for victory. Heh, heh.

Farthest from home that I have ever played Munchkin: 8,624.3 miles, in Canberra, Australia.

Farthest from home that I have ever played Munchkin *if you think about it like a munchkin:* 4,200 miles, give or take, which would be the distance to Canberra if you measure straight through the earth.

EXCESSIVELY RANDOM STUFF

Number of major gaming awards won by the Munchkin *series:* Eight, as I count from our page at www.sjgames.com/general/awards.html, including the Origins Award for Best Traditional Card Game of 2001, when *Munchkin* was first released.

Number of major awards or other significant recognitions that Munchkin *has received for its social and educational value:* Zero.

Number of times somebody has said to me "I like that game!" when they saw me wearing my Munchkin *shirt:* Too many to count. It was amazing the first time it happened.

Who am I kidding? It's still amazing! That's one reason I like wearing *Munchkin* shirts.

Books written about Munchkin: One. You're reading it. Hi!

Highest price ever paid for a Munchkin *card:* $1,031.78.

Munchkin has never been a collectible card game, and we have never deliberately created great rarity. But just once we permitted a convention to do a fully official *Munchkin* card. It was "Heart of the Anomaly," a *Star Munchkin* promo created by Linucon 2004 in Austin, as a tribute to guest (and *Munchkin* player) Wil Wheaton. They didn't print very many, and that was a long time ago . . . so when one appeared on eBay, the bidding went high. (And that one wasn't even signed by Wil. If he signs the card, it gives an extra +1!)

Highest price ever paid by an individual to appear on a Munchkin *card:* $4,000, by Steven Dengler of www.dracogen.com, at a charity auction to benefit Child's Play. Thanks, Steven!

There have also been several four-figure donations from groups of two or three bidders at Irish game conventions (which have an unmatched reputation for charity giving; for more on that, see Colm Lundberg's essay in this volume) and the Lucca Comics & Games Show. Card auctions show up at various events, usually without warning, benefiting causes such as children's hospitals. If you want a munchkin-y version of your face, or a friend's, to show up on a card, this is the way to do it.

Number of Munchkin-*themed weddings that we know about:* Three, plus one proposal via homemade one-of-a-kind *Munchkin* card.

What the foil hat and socks are made of: 10.

FAN RECORDS

We can't substantiate these. Who do you think we are, *Guinness*? But fans have written us to claim the following records:

Most successive school days playing Munchkin: 90.

Matt Ehler: "For a full semester, my mates and I played a minimum of one game of *Munchkin* a day, often two. This is 18 weeks of five school days per week." (So, Matt, you were slacking off on the weekends?)

Most players in a Munchkin *game:* 18.

Jeff Kochosky: "A number of years ago, at a convention in CT (ConnCon), I ran a game of *Epic Munchkin* that had 18 players involved. We used every base set and expansion through *Super Munchkin 2.* I had to walk around the tables distributing the cards, because they couldn't be kept in one place. The game lasted about 6 hours."

Second-most players in a Munchkin *game:* 15.

John LaRoche: "It took place last year at the Fantasy Gaming Conclave . . . a massive four-table game that involved original *Munchkin* and *Munchkin Cthulhu* using dungeons for both. Portals that replaced a dungeon in play would cause that player to go to a different table. The first player at any table to reach level 20 would win for all tables. If 15 players isn't a record, just wait until the FGC this year. I'll have the *Zombie* dungeons to add to the fun!"

Youngest player: 4.

Neil McLellan: "I have played *Munchkin* with my two daughters, 4 years old and 5 years old . . . Daddy lost. The two girls, Hannah and

Lana, shared a win due to Elven shenanigans." (Neil sent unspeakably cute photos.)

Highest combat value in a monster stack: 156.

Adam Ford: "Yes, the monsters won." (Former *Munchkin* Baron Lenny found a claim of 193 on a message board, but it was several years old and we could not confirm it.)

Longest game of Munchkin *(with the same players):* Seven hours.

Steve Mandel: "We played an all-sets, all-expansions *Epic Munchkin* game once. For six of us, it took seven hours, but someone finally got to level 20 and won."

Longest game of Munchkin *(with rotating players):* 12 hours.

Scot Ryder: "I was a MIB when *Munchkin* came out and was heading to DragonCon that year. On Friday I started a *Munchkin* demo around 8 P.M. in the open gaming area. We played *Munchkin*. And played *Munchkin*. And played *Munchkin*. Players rotated in and out but the 'demo' lasted over 12 hours. It was then that I knew *Munchkin* was going to be a huge hit, though I couldn't have anticipated how huge!"

SO HOW DOES IT ALL ADD UP?

I am so tempted to total all those "significant numbers" and claim that is the true meaning of *Munchkin*. But if the silly game adds up to a good time for you, I'm happy. ✴

Steve Jackson has been designing games for almost 40 years and has no plans to stop. He may be blamed for *Munchkin*, *Illuminati*, the *GURPS* roleplaying system, *Ogre*, *Car Wars*, and *Zombie Dice*. He is either a citizen of the Internet or a Texan, depending on who's asking.

MUNCHKIN DILEMMA

You may either: Go up a level and draw two extra Treasure cards when helping someone defeat a monster; or you may add Death to Bad Stuff of one monster and take one extra card while Looting the Body if the munchkin(s) facing the monster die.

To Backstab or Not to Backstab

Game Theory and the *Munchkin* Dilemma

Andrew Zimmerman Jones

We've all been there, standing next to our Warrior buddy (for lack of a better term) as he decides to kick down the door. There, on the other side, is an Unspeakably Awful Indescribable Horror.

The Warrior turns to us, asking for help. We have a moment – a heartbeat – to decide before the beast is upon us. In the words of the classic song, should we stay or should we go now? And, while running away, should we cast a spell to enlarge the Horror so it eats our friend?

This is the classic dilemma that faces players of *Munchkin*.

Loaded Die: A Winning Strategy

On one hand, my goal in the overall game is to beat my buddy, so I want to watch him get devoured by the Horror. As for the other hand . . . actually, this helps me out. I guess there is no other hand!

Well, that was easy. Maybe this isn't a dilemma after all.

What's that? He's willing to bribe me? Treasure? I suppose I can reconsider the situation.

To figure out the best strategy, this shrieking geek looks to the mathematical field of game theory. The goal of game theory is to quantify the possible outcomes of a game, then determine which actions provide what payoff (either a gain or a loss). The game theorist is often able to develop an overall strategy that results in maximized rewards or minimized losses.

A game where the positive and negative payoffs, the gains and losses, exactly balance out is called a *zero-sum game.*

Assume that a Wizard and a Cleric are gambling at the tavern after their adventuring is done. They've been kicking in doors and looting all evening. So now they're playing a simple game. Each places a flat bet of 1 gold piece, then they each flip over a card. The higher card takes the 2 gold pieces. There are three possible outcomes to this basic game:

	Wizard payoff	Cleric payoff
Cleric card high	−1 gold	+1 gold
Wizard card high	+1 gold	−1 gold
Wizard & Cleric tie	0 gold	0 gold

The amount of money one player wins is precisely balanced by the amount of money that the other player loses. Each combination of payoffs (each row in the table, in this case) adds up to zero, so this

counts as a zero-sum game. It's a fair game and there's no strategy that might give either player an advantage over the other.

That's not always the case.

At another table in the tavern, the Warrior and the Thief are playing a different game, one that the Thief has only recently taught to the Warrior. In this game, each player puts a two-sided coin down on the table, choosing whether to place it heads or tails. As the Thief carefully explains, the payoffs are as follows:

	Warrior heads	**Warrior tails**
Thief heads	*Warrior:* −1 gold *Thief:* +1 gold	*Warrior:* 0 gold *Thief:* 0 gold
Thief tails	*Warrior:* +1 gold *Thief:* −1 gold	*Warrior:* −1 gold *Thief:* +1 gold

This again is a zero-sum game, since the payoff combinations in each cell adds up to zero. But in this game there is a strategy that favors the Thief. If you add up the Thief's payouts in a given row, you see that the sum when he plays heads is +1 gold and the sum when he plays tails is 0. If the Thief plays only heads, there is no chance that he will lose any gold pieces. He might very rarely switch over to tails just to throw the Warrior off the scam, but aside from this, his best strategy is to always go heads.

The Warrior's situation is worse. Considering the sum of his payouts in the two columns, playing heads yields a sum of 0 gold while playing tails gives a sum of −1 gold. Playing tails is an overall losing strategy for the Warrior, so he will have to develop some sort of "mixed strategy" that involves playing heads some portion of the time and tails some portion of the time.

But because the Thief is playing a pure strategy of selecting only heads, the Warrior's mixed strategy is never going to make up the difference, and he will lose money while never gaining any. Presumably, he will eventually figure out that the Thief is selecting nothing but heads, but not

until he has lost at least a few gold pieces. The game is rigged so that the best the Warrior can hope for is to minimize his losses. The only winning strategy for the Warrior is to not agree to play the Thief's game!

Just because something is zero sum doesn't actually mean it is fair. That was, after all, why the Thief suggested this game in the first place. The Warrior would be better off clobbering the little sneak with an Eleven-Foot Pole and looting his body for the evening's drink money.

HELP ME OUT HERE: COOPERATION STRATEGIES

Cooperation took a while to show up in game theory, or in games for that matter. Many classic games don't incorporate any element of cooperation at all. It is never a good strategic choice to cooperate with your opponent in checkers, chess, or backgammon, for example.

These games still count as zero-sum pursuits, though. If a move in checkers results in someone taking two pieces, then that player has gotten a +2 piece advantage while the other player has gotten a –2 piece disadvantage. This holds true even when you take into account the ability to gain the impressive-sounding title of king. Quantifying the value of the pieces is even trickier in chess, due to so many impressive-sounding titles, but it still counts as zero sum. There may be strategic reasons to take a momentary disadvantage to gain a greater long-term advantage for the win, but the benefits and losses of individual moves still result in these strictly competitive games also being considered zero sum.

It's not a coincidence that one of the first competitive games where I ever encountered the idea of strategic cooperation was a non-zero-sum design. It's a little-known boardgame that involves the buying and selling of properties, the building of houses and hotels, and the raiding of municipal funds by greedy oligarchs. In this game, the strategy isn't merely to crush one's enemies, but to make deals with the other players. You have to give the other player something that he or she wants, but try to tailor the deal in such a way that you come out ahead.

Because players can gain money from the bank, it's actually possible to gain payoffs that aren't zero sum – most clearly evident when two players collude with each other to stomp a powerful third player. There's a reason, after all, that this sort of behavior is (sometimes) illegal in real-world business practices: because the sum of two players working together is truly greater than any individual player could hope to be.

I haven't played that game in quite some time, mostly because I'm still waiting for a *Munchkin*-based adaptation.

After the Thief awakens the next morning, head ringing from the beating he took, he limps back to his companions only to find them standing around a potion merchant's wagon. The group is getting gear for their upcoming dungeon raid. The merchant sells mostly Electric Radioactive Acid Potions (complete with necessary hazmat gear), but he has one vial of the coveted Pollymorph Potion. The merchant announces that he will begin an auction for the Pollymorph Potion in a few minutes, but there's a catch in this auction: everyone who bids has to pay their final bid, though the runners-up will get an Electric Radioactive Acid Potion for their trouble. A nearby paladin is on hand to make sure that no one agrees to the terms and then tries to weasel out of the deal.

The competitive strategy in this situation is obvious: everyone should go pawn off their useless junk so they can begin bidding on that Pollymorph Potion, doing whatever they can to gain it. It is, after all, the potion that they all *really* want.

But there's an obvious problem here. If they all go for the Polly-morph Potion, they'll be outbidding one another. And, given that they're something of a spiteful bunch, they realistically know that things will get out of hand and they will all ultimately lose a lot of money, with only one of them potentially getting the Pollymorph Potion . . . assuming they aren't *all* outbid by a smug, smartly dressed Bard who has just walked up to the wagon to join in the auction.

Instead of focusing exclusively on their individual goal – the desire to get the Pollymorph Potion – let's say that the adventurers instead take a step back and consider the group's overall goal. All four adventurers would like to buy a potion and have money left over for other gear. That will not happen if they all focus on the Pollymorph Potion.

There is another strategy available, though: if they all can agree to buy the Electric Radioactive Acid Potion, they won't get into a futile bidding war, and they can go on about their day with a powerful new potion among their gear.

And it works fine, so long as no one breaks ranks and deviates from the plan.

KILL THE HIRELING:
DEFECTION AND BETRAYAL

Once the plan is set in motion, there's always the possibility of some-one deviating from it. This is called a *defection* from a cooperative strategy. While the other three adventurers are walking through the market looking for other gear, the Thief could decide to circle back and join in the auction for the Pollymorph Potion. But if any of the other adventurers notice that the Thief is breaking the agreement, they might decide to do so as well. Indeed, being petty and spiteful little munchkins, they will.

Game theorists have considered the consequences of this lack of cooperation in a classic game theory problem that's become known as

the Prisoner's Dilemma. For our example, let's say the night watch grabs a couple of adventurers, a female Warrior and a female Cleric, accused of having stolen a nobleman's Staff of Napalm. (She's a Cleric, not a priest.) Witnesses saw them breaking a window in the nobleman's house, but there are no witnesses to the theft itself. Neither has the staff with her.

Without a confession, they'll both spend a month in jail, at the very least, for having broken a window. Also, the nobleman wants one thing: the return of his Staff of Napalm. He's offered a deal: if both confess and tell him the location of the staff, he'll ask that they only be sentenced to three months apiece. If one confesses and the other does not, however, the night watch will have the evidence they need to send the one who doesn't confess to jail for a year. The one who confesses will be set free as soon as the nobleman gets the staff back.

Oh, and the one who gets ratted out without confessing will get a finger chopped off.

It's a harsh world out there.

Again, we can look at the possible payoffs in a table:

	Cleric keeps quiet (cooperates)	Cleric confesses (defects)
Warrior keeps quiet (cooperates)	*Cleric:* 1 month in jail *Warrior:* 1 month in jail	*Cleric:* Goes free *Warrior:* 12 months in jail and loses a finger
Warrior confesses (defects)	*Cleric:* 12 months in jail and loses a finger *Warrior:* Goes free	*Cleric:* 3 months in jail *Warrior:* 3 months in jail

The Warrior learned about life from her brother, a Warrior who once got fleeced gambling with a Thief in a tavern, so she thinks carefully about all of her options. She realizes that no matter what the Cleric does, it's always in her own best interest to confess. If the Cleric keeps quiet, then confessing takes the Warrior from a one-month sentence to freedom. If both she and the Cleric confess, then the Warrior's sentence will be reduced from a year to three months, plus she gets to keep all her fingers. She's no idiot, so she decides to act in her best interest and confess.

The Cleric considers her options, as well. Her best strategy is to confess and hope that the Warrior keeps quiet, gaining her freedom at the expense of the Warrior. (She *really* is not a very good Cleric, but figures she can repent later.) If the Warrior does confess, then they both spend three months in jail, but at least everyone keeps all their fingers. Like the Warrior, she realizes that her best strategy is to confess.

Then the Cleric has an epiphany. Perhaps it comes in a vision from her deity. When they both confess, when they both act in a way that is clearly in their self-interest, the result is three months in jail apiece. But if they had both acted *against* their best interest, and held true to each other, their outcome would have been one month in jail apiece.

With this realization, the Cleric is renewed in her understanding of her mission in the service of her benevolent deity – to spread the good word of peace and cooperation throughout the land, so that people will live in accord with each other, attaining the best outcomes for society.

When the night watchmen return, the Cleric promptly confesses and tells them where the Staff of Napalm is. She may wish for a world where everyone can be trusted to act against her or his own best interest, for the good of the whole, but she's not willing to bet her finger on it.

Mutilate the Bodies: Cooperation in *Munchkin*

The Prisoner's Dilemma may seem like an abstract, highly contrived situation, but it has powerful implications in game theory, economics, and dungeon crawling.

Consider two companies competing against each other in the gaming industry. Zero-sum thinking says they must constantly work against each other, trying to gain an advantage.

For the non-zero-sum innovator, these competing gaming companies can benefit from mutual cooperation. They could create a hybrid product that uses the mechanics of a game system owned by one company, skinned with the intellectual property of another to create something new. Fans of both games will obviously love it, as will many fans of one game who had never played the other. Such cooperation benefits both parties, and also the gamers who love them, as shown by the existence of *Munchkin Pathfinder Deluxe* and *Munchkin Panic*.

After all of these side quests and adventures, consider again an adventurer (let's go with a classless female Halfling) standing in the dungeon when her Warrior buddy kicks down a door, sees the Horror unspeakably before him, and looks over for help. He imploringly appeals to the Halfling's friendship and sense of decency.

When that fails, he offers her a bribe.

This is a scenario that I have dubbed the *Munchkin* Dilemma. In one very important way, it's significantly different from the Prisoner's Dilemma: defection is not normally an option for the Warrior, only for the other players.

The Halfling can either cooperate or defect, and the defection can take several forms. She could simply refuse to help. Even more significantly, she (or any other player) could actively work against the Warrior in the fight, using Monster Enhancers to guarantee his defeat.

The *Munchkin* Dilemma is much more difficult to quantify than the cases we've looked at so far, because two types of payoffs are involved. For the Warrior, victory against the Unspeakably Awful Indescribable Horror means he gains a level and four treasure cards, less any cards offered in a bribe. If the Warrior doesn't get help, he will lose. If he can't run away, he'll end up being killed and losing all his stuff. Everyone else in the party will loot the body.

The lack of defection by the Warrior makes the table a little different, but it's still helpful in quantifying the various factors at play, depending on whether the Warrior can gain an ally or not in the fight.

	Payoffs
Help the Warrior (cooperate)	*Warrior:* +1 level, some treasure cards *Ally:* Some treasure cards (+1 level if an Elf) *Other Players:* Tears and sorrow
Don't help the Warrior (defect)	*Warrior:* No levels or treasure. Run away. Possible death. *Other Players:* Possible looting of the body, if Warrior dies

The chance of any player cooperating in the fight comes down to negotiating what "some treasure cards" means. If the Warrior is offering to hand over his Tuba of Charm, the situation is very different than if he's offering up his Staff of Napalm to a Wizard. Or the Warrior may offer the possible ally their choice of the treasure cards. If so, the person being asked to aid the Warrior is gambling on what cards will come up as treasure, determining how many of them he will get, and who gets to pick those cards.

The number of players is also a factor, because in a two-player game you are the Warrior's only opportunity to avoid loss (and possible death). But if there are other people at the table and you insist on getting all four cards, the Warrior might be willing to turn you down, banking on the idea that someone else will help him for only two cards. Or, if everyone in the game drives too hard a bargain, he might just risk his chance to run away.

All the number crunching and odds figuring can be thrown out the window if the Warrior is willing to risk death just to spite other players.

Really Impressive Title:
Reputation and Repeated Play

In the story of the staff-stealing Warrior and Cleric, the Cleric guaranteed that she would keep her finger by confessing – thus betraying her Warrior friend. She did so because she was fairly certain that the Warrior would *also* confess.

But the Cleric could have held to her convictions and said nothing, believing that it was nobler to remain true to her ally. (Assuming she has such convictions. Given that we are talking about an ally in stealing a Staff of Napalm, this particular Cleric continues to make some extremely skewed value judgments.) The Warrior had no similar convictions, so she confessed, betraying the Cleric.

A couple of years later, after the Cleric has gotten out of jail and regenerated her finger, she and the Warrior are again brought before the night watch for some crime.  They are offered a similar deal.

This time, the Warrior has a piece of information that she didn't have before: she believes that she *can* trust the Cleric to keep quiet, because she's done it before. Everything she knows about the Cleric makes her absolutely certain that the Cleric will remain quiet this

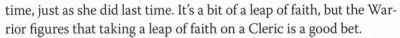

time, just as she did last time. It's a bit of a leap of faith, but the Warrior figures that taking a leap of faith on a Cleric is a good bet.

Keep in mind that it's still in the Warrior's immediate best interest to betray the Cleric. With betrayal, the Warrior gets released that very night instead of serving a month of jail time. It would seem like the Warrior should betray the Cleric again.

Mathematicians have tried to figure out the best strategy for approaching the Prisoner's Dilemma. In competitions, different strategies have been set against each other in rounds of competition. The "winning" strategy is the one that gets the least amount of jail time (or other penalty) throughout the course of the competition. Some strategies include always cooperating, always betraying, or randomly choosing betrayal or cooperation. These strategies are not particularly successful, though, as they have weaknesses that can be exploited by other strategies.

The strategy that proves the most successful is called Tit-For-Tat. When it encounters a new player, its first move is always to cooperate. Then, from that point on, if it encounters a player that it has played before, it copies the action that the other player made before. It doesn't hold grudges for past slights (beyond the last one), it isn't the first one to defect, but it also doesn't ignore past betrayals entirely (as the Cleric seems willing to do). These three traits make it the most successful strategy in these repeated-play competitions.

Tit-For-Tat isn't a perfect strategy. Other strategies can defeat it. In the most obvious example, if a Warrior using Tit-For-Tat were in a Prisoner's Dilemma with a Thief who always betrays, the Warrior would begin by cooperating and be betrayed on the first round. On every other round, both the Warrior and Thief would betray each other, but the Warrior still lost on the first round, so the Tit-For-Tat strategy loses to the Always Betray strategy.

But the Always Betray strategy doesn't do well in these competitions overall. Most strategies quickly figure out that the player is always betraying, and that reputation causes it to suffer over the course of repeated plays. Tit-For-Tat is flexible enough that it comes out ahead on average against more strategies.

The most important element of Tit-For-Tat is that reputation matters. Strategies that don't take reputation into account always suffer for it. The Warrior's decision needs to account for the fact that she will gain a reputation as someone who betrays her friends when it counts.

Reputation matters in the *Munchkin* Dilemma, as well. It's likely that someone in that group is quickly going to prove to be far more mercenary than the other players, insisting on high payments for offering any help. Players who need help are likely to favor those who take a more, "Yeah, sure, I'll help you out for just one treasure card" position.

Over repeated plays, being picked to help more often is likely to provide a greater advantage than rarely helping in exchange for massive bribes. A Halfling who is always willing to help for just a single treasure card can get several extra cards over the course of the game. The Elf, who gets a level bonus for assisting, will often help other players without taking any cards. Either of these players is more likely to be asked to help more often than the Warrior.

Part of the reason *Munchkin* is so much fun is that its play options and rewards are so diverse. They cannot be reduced to easily quantified payoffs and losses. Game theory helps us at least rule out the worst strategies. For those who haven't learned this lesson any other way, it can teach that being a continual jerk is not a good strategy. It can teach us that ignoring, or even rewarding, bad behavior has negative consequences.

But it cannot offer guaranteed paths to success in every single situation. Even the best strategy, such as Tit-For-Tat, has its limitations. At times, reputation must be sacrificed for a truly great move.

Even those of us who enjoy a fairly light hearted, non-cutthroat version of *Munchkin* occasionally find ourselves in a position where we've agreed to help a level 7 Wizard fight a Bullrog in exchange for four treasure cards. Then, as we resolve the combat, we realize that we can use a Pollymorph Potion to get our treasure cards but prevent our buddy from getting two levels.

Sometimes, the circumstances just call for a good backstabbing. ✳

Andrew Zimmerman Jones was given a copy of *Chez Geek* as a housewarming present when he bought his home. Though he played *Munchkin* with friends, it took him an inexplicably long time to buy his own copy. While building up to the purchase, he was known to stand for hours in front of the *Munchkin* display at his local gaming store, contemplating which version was the perfect one. His wife eventually took pity on him and bought the core set. In between games, Andrew is a full-time freelance writer focusing on science, education, and popular culture. He is the Physics Expert at About.com and co-author of *String Theory for Dummies*, as well as a contributing editor of *Black Gate* fantasy magazine. His work has appeared on a number of blogs and in popular-culture books, including *Beyond the Wall* and *Inside Joss' Dollhouse.*

PUNishment

Use during any combat. For each pun you can make in one minute, you may add +1 to either side.

MADNESS IN 168 EASY STEPS

Andrew Hackard

The most frequent question I am asked by *Munchkin* fans is, "How do you come up with all those cards?" (The second-most frequent question is, "Some of the jokes in your game are just awful. Aren't you ever ashamed?" I love you too, Mom.) In the interest of total transparency, therefore, and on behalf of the entire *Munchkin* team, let me offer a window into the design process of a new *Munchkin* game. Our new and wholly fictitious *Munchkin* game is to be called *Munchkin Baroque*, a whimsical contest centered around backstabbing, double-dealing, and monster slaying in the blood-drenched world of 17th-century chamber music.

In other words . . . we'll be Bach!

A PREEMPTIVE DIGRESSION

But, of course, I've gotten ahead of myself, so let me back up a moment. Coming up with the theme of a new *Munchkin* set is rarely as easy as waltzing into a meeting, throwing down the *Brandenburg Concerti*, and waltzing back out. (For one thing, very few of Bach's works are in 3/4 time.) Deciding on the next *Munchkin* game is a discussion often encompassing several conversations over the span of weeks. We ask ourselves such vital questions as:

* Does this have wide appeal, or are we just writing this to amuse ourselves?
* Do we, personally, know enough about the subject to write 168 cards without making unnecessary asses of ourselves?
* Is it inherently funny? If not, can we make it funny?
* Seriously, guys, is anyone going to buy this game?

In this case, let's assume we've asked those questions and are proceeding with *Munchkin Baroque* anyway. Otherwise, I have to come up with a new example, and I'm already behind deadline.[1]

FIRST STEPS

Once we've decided on a theme, we have to establish the basic features of the set. Most *Munchkin* games have two possible character traits, such as classes and races or mojos and powers. Deciding what to call the traits is sometimes as simple as, "Let's just go with classes and races and break for lunch." Some sets, however, have suffered a more difficult birth, leading to statements like, "If they look like powers and they work like powers, why aren't we calling them powers? And if we

---

[1] Deadlines got their name in Roman times, when emperors expected their speechwriters to have their impromptu remarks ready no later than one hour before it was time for the unscheduled speech. The only way for a writer to keep his job – and his head – was to write quickly and accurately, thus using his pen to hold the sword at bay. Or so Steve tells me, and he's my boss, so I believe him completely.

do, we don't have to write a bunch of new rules and we can break for lunch."[2]

We generally have a good idea of how many monsters (of various levels), types of treasures (headgear, armor, and so on), and screw-your-buddy cards (everything else) go into a set. Steve has a skeleton document that he or I can use when we're just starting to write the cards for a game, so the easy part is done. (Writing 168 jokes? That's the challenge.) We'll vary the formula where the needs of a set seem to demand it – or when we feel like it – but most *Munchkin* sets are pretty much fleshed out from the same skeleton. This is good, because it means that when people buy a new set, it is comforting and familiar and they feel good about giving us their rent money. Also, it saves us a lot of work, and we're all about that. Too much work, and this will start to feel like a real job.[3]

COMING UP WITH ALL THOSE AWFUL JOKES

The mainstay of many elementary school classrooms is the process of brainstorming. This is where everyone gets around a big table, huffs dry-erase markers for a few minutes, and then starts spitting out the dumbest, least practical solutions to whatever intractable problem has stalled work that day.[4] No idea is too stupid, implausible, or offensive, and no one is allowed to be critical of anyone else's harebrained offerings during the brainstorming session. That comes later.

---

[2] *Game Design Tip:* Start all development meetings five minutes before lunch.

[3] Sometimes people have the mistaken impression that Steve and I just sit around playing games all day. That is wildly inaccurate. I try to set aside at least an hour each workday for something besides games, and I think Steve may be up to *two* hours. We hope you appreciate our sacrifice.

[4] I may be confusing elementary school with college. It was a long time ago.

Like many other megacorpora-
tions, we at *Munchkin* Central have
implemented brainstorming as a
vital part of our development cycle.
However, we've made a few modifi-
cations. First, we've done away with
that "every idea has value" crap. You
cannot expect several people who
have been picked for their skill with
words, honed on the whetstone of
snark, to stay quiet when someone[5]

suggests Love Handels as a treasure in *Munchkin Baroque*. We've
tried, we really have, but keeping your opinion to yourself after someone coughs up a hairball of an idea like that one is tantamount to
holding back a sneeze whose time has come – your eyes bug out, your
cheeks inflate, and you may as well let it loose, because by that point
everyone else knows what you're thinking and you may hurt yourself
if you don't just share it.

I've only been writing *Munchkin* cards professionally for seven
years. Steve's been doing this since the game launched in 2001. What
amazes me, looking at over a decade of Steve's work, is how consis-
tently he has hit the mark. It makes me very happy when one of my
cards makes Steve say, "That joke is awful. I never would have thought
of that." It's an unusual bit of praise, but our job is far from usual.

One of the most challenging parts of this process is avoiding rep-
etition of a joke we've already used (unless we're doing it on purpose).
With over 6,000 *Munchkin* cards so far, the bottoms of some pretty
gnarly barrels have been scraped right through. Each new theme
brings a whole new set of pun barrels to tap (*Munchkin Baroque*, for
instance, has a monster called Chopin Tiger, Haydn Dragon[6]), but

---

[5] Okay, me. I'm not proud.
[6] Well, it does now.

we've written so many cards now that many of the obvious jokes have already been used, genre tropes be damned. It's a good thing that the English language is endlessly abusable, for abuse it we do. I thought that I was an expert punster, but working under Steve has made me thoroughly incorrigible. Luckily, Steve is happy to incorrige me. Under his tutelage, I have shed all inhibitions and taste, and it has freed me to write cards that really should be banned under international law.[7]

With three creative, snarky people (Steve, me, and John Kovalic – more about him later) all involved in the card design process, we're pretty ruthless about rejecting ideas that are too obscure, trite, or just uninspired. Eventually, we end up with 168 cards that are ready to go to the next circle of Game Design Hell: playtesting.

PLAYTESTING IN PROGRESS: CHECK YOUR SELF-WORTH AT THE DOOR

The best (worst) jokes in the world can't save a *Munchkin* set if it doesn't work as a game. Playtesting is where, with the assistance of brave volunteers, we discover all the places where we screwed up. It's a bit like crowdsourced freelance editing, except that people get paid in pizza, not money.[8] In the case of *Munchkin Baroque*, it's as though Mozart let the orchestra dissect and revise his newest symphony while they're playing it. Playtesting is nerve-racking, frustrating, disheartening, often maddening, and utterly necessary.

Among the things we ask our playtesters to check are:

* The balance of the various classes (powers, etc.). Do they work together well? If there's one class that everyone – or no

---

[7] My parents are so proud.

[8] On second thought, it's *exactly* like freelance editing. (Just ask Our Humble Editor.)

one – wants to play, that tells us we need to adjust them all so they're more or less equally desirable.

* Same question with our treasures. Some of them are qualitatively better than others, but we usually find ways to balance this out, either by increasing the temptation to sell those cards for levels or by limiting their use so that players have to decide when to pull the trigger on an especially nifty card. Unlike with the classes, however, we want a bit of imbalance. That creates envy, which drives the interpersonal conflict that makes *Munchkin* so charming.

* High and low points. Are there any cards that stand out as especially good, especially nasty, or especially blah? If playtesters say, "I have no idea why I would ever play this card" (or the opposite: "I would play this card every game if I had it"), that tells us we may need to go back and adjust things. Of course, sometimes we decide the effect is rare enough, or funny enough, that we can leave it alone.

* Clarity. What is confusing or just seems kind of wonky? This open-ended question has led to some of our most insightful playtest comments.[9] It turns out that when you give people a chance to tell you what they don't like, they're often willing to take it. At great length. For example, in *Munchkin Baroque*, I had the brilliant idea to create a curse card called "Deaf Composer," which required the victim to put his fingers in his ears and hum Beethoven until the start of his next turn. This card was, to put it mildly, unpopular. I eventually replaced it with a monster derived from the Ring Cycle: "Siegfried et Roi." This was also panned, on the specious grounds that Siegfried was German, not French. It's a hard life, being a game designer.

---

[9] Usually prefaced with "WTF," which I am told stands for "What's That From?" or possibly "Why's That Funny?"

* Humor. Which jokes were especially funny? Which jokes weren't? This is one of our checks for obscurity, which we ignore at our own peril. If you see Steve at a convention, ask him about the "Filthy Geats" card. It required a working knowledge of both *Beowulf* and George Michael, and the insight[10]

to make the connection. Or, to pick on myself, the card named "Bridle Shower" – obviously, that's a shady character who shows bridles. The art helps that card, but even so, it's quite a stretch and makes people read the title twice, which is at least once too often.

Our first group of playtesters is the *Munchkin* Brain Trust. These loyal fans have proven their dedication to the *Munchkin* game by offering up thousands of words of opinions (solicited and not) about every published set, and have repeatedly demonstrated their deep insight into the underpinnings of *Munchkin* and how it is put together. This makes them invaluable to the design process.[11] Their work has saved Steve and me from publishing unintentionally stupid rules more times than I want to think about. ("What do you mean, *Munchkin Baroque* shouldn't include keytars?")

The real test of a new *Munchkin* game, however, comes when we take it out into the public and let them get their cheesy fingerprints all

---

[10] Sure, we'll call it that.

[11] Also massive pains in the butt. Just like real butt pain, however, they keep us from getting too comfortable.

over it.[12] When we introduce a game-in-progress to the undifferentiated masses of distracted parents, arrogant teenagers, novice players, and (shudder) rules lawyers, we get suggestions from every type of gamer, all designed to help us make the game better. We also, rarely, get the kind of raw feedback that's usually reserved for the abyss that is a YouTube comment thread. The first lesson Steve taught me is, "It's not personal," and that is a maxim I hold on to when I feel my lip quivering after reading a brutal takedown of some cherished idea.

We credit our playtesters who make useful, helpful comments – or comments that make us laugh so hard that bystanders summon medical attention – so many of them take the time to do a good job. Thanks, playtesters; your assistance is more crucial than you know. Just ignore our tears of blood as you tell us what we did wrong.

IT'S HARD TO MAKE ART LOOK THIS EASY

Once a new *Munchkin* game has run the playtesting gauntlet and our wounds have been salved, it's time to transmute our low-rent playtest cards into the real thing. At this point, we turn matters over to John Kovalic and his talented (if overworked) drawing arm.

It is impossible to overvalue John's contributions to *Munchkin*. It's his art that people see when they pick up a *Munchkin* box, his art that appears on many of the cards,[13] and often his art that takes a

---

[12] *Pro tip:* Stash wet wipes in your playtest kit. Convention-center nacho-cheese-sauce product makes the cards in your spiffy prototype much harder to shuffle. Card sleeves are a must.

[13] With the exception of the occasional guest card and the even rarer exception of the entire set drawn by another artist, John has drawn every *Munchkin* card to date. That's more than 5,000 game illustrations drawn by a single hand, and we have hundreds more in the works as I write this. Plus, John has drawn illustrations for *Illuminati: New World Order*, *Chez Geek*, and even some non-SJ Games games. He's been drawing a comic strip turned comic book turned webcomic, *Dork Tower*,

middle-of-the-road joke and elevates it to the sublime. (Any failures of sublimation remain the responsibility of the designers; John can't save every card. He's a genius, not a superhero.[14])

With the benefit of decades of experience, John often knows what works, artistically, far better than we mere wordsmiths. We have learned to listen intently when John explains why our idea for a card illustration is difficult, or even

Hi, I'm DED

just inferior, because he's almost always right. The best times, though, are when John takes a pedestrian art spec (short for "specification," the brief description of what should fill the box marked *ART GOES HERE*) and gives us a drawing far better than what we had envisioned. My officemates have learned the precise laugh that says, more clearly than words, "John has done it again."

Even John's rare mistakes are gifted. We wrote a card a couple of years ago for which we specified a zombie head flying through the air. For some reason, John got fixated on the idea that it was a zombie horse's head[15] and drew it that way. This gave us a really funny piece of art that was not at all what we'd imagined for the card. We didn't reject the art; we realized that we just had art for which the appropriate text had not yet been written. In this case, the obvious answer was to

---

for well over a decade now. Oh, yeah, he designs games, too. And he does all this while he and his wife, Judith, raise a delightful young daughter. Between you and me, I think he's a cyborg.

[14] As far as I know. It occurs to me, however, that I've never seen him and Aquaman together. . . .

[15] Mario Puzo, call your agent.

write a card called "Mister Ded." As a bonus, that one art suggestion generated two cards. Efficiency!

Writing good specs is an art unto itself, one I am still working to perfect. A regular feature of my workday is a call or email from John in which he identifies a piece of art he's not sure about or explains why my idea is unworkable. ("Andrew, I know it would be funny to draw the entire cast of *Amadeus* for *Munchkin Baroque*, but I only have about three square inches to work with. Can we maybe just do Salieri this time?") John is patient, kind, erudite, and one of the funniest people I know. He's pulled our butts out of the fire more times than I care to think about.[16]

For *Munchkin Baroque*, we have created a new running art gag: all the characters are wearing white wigs. This may or may not be historically accurate,[17] but it does act as a unifying element, a peg for John to hang all his art on. This saves us a bit of time, which is at a premium by this point in the design process. We usually give John about two months to complete a full *Munchkin* set. This reserves all of us lots of time for collaboration, revisions, and the inevitable "Wait, John, we had a better idea" last-minute emails that are the delight of his existence. To be blunt about it, it's a miracle he hasn't stabbed us all with his beloved fine-tip pens by now.

Once the art starts coming in, it goes over to our talented production team for coloring and layout. Fitting too-long text[18] onto a small card and leaving enough room to show off the art is a challenge, one they meet brilliantly. They also get to lay out the rules, the box

---

[16] Some fans have told me that anyone could do what John does. Maybe one or two of them actually could . . . but I'm not holding my breath. That's kind of like saying that anyone who owns *Garage Band* could write a symphony.

[17] We do a surprising amount of research – or at least *Wikipedia* surfing – for some of our *Munchkin* design. But that doesn't mean we are averse to anachronism in the service of a good joke. Hell, even a mediocre one. In the conflict between "funny" and "true," funny almost always wins.

[18] Steve and I do like our adverbs.

(designing the box is a subject worth its own essay), and any ancillary materials we decide to include. There are close to 200 individual pieces in a *Munchkin* set, and the production team builds every one of them.

WE'LL FIX IT IN POSTPRODUCTION

Once the layout work is completed, the game goes to prepress for a final set of checks before it goes to print. This is our last opportunity to fix things without spending a whole lot of money, so it's a critical stage – and one for which we never allot as much time as we really want. As deadlines slide earlier in the process – not an inevitability, but it does tend to happen – you create a comical "must get all the work done *now*" pileup at the final stages.[19] A somewhat startling number of mistakes, both typographical and conceptual, get caught at these final stages ("Did you really mean to include a keytar in a Renaissance orchestra?"), so we dare not stint on it. This can lead to frantic phone calls to our printer that include these words: "I know you said this was a drop-dead date, but what's the *real* drop-dead . . . ? Oh."

Once our prepress checker is satisfied that the set is as good as it's going to get, everything goes off to the manufacturer. From a design standpoint the game is complete and we just have to wait for it to start appearing on store shelves. Yay, the work is done!

Except, not.

"We'll fix it in postproduction" is a Hollywood cliché, but sometimes it's

---

[19] Comical if you aren't the person trying to finish the damn game, of course. If you are that person, substitute "infuriating." Also, I'm sorry.

literally true. Computers are complex, and something that looks fine on the screens in our office can turn to gibberish when it's set for physical production. This final proof stage is our chance to recognize those glitches (usually to a chorus of howls and cursing) and stomp them before they reach print. We don't always catch everything – every publisher has at least one good story about The Horrid Mistake That Got Printed. I have a few myself, and I'm not about to reveal them here.[20]

Okay, just one. In *Munchkin Baroque*, I wrote a monster card called "Dirty Oboes," which has the poor maligned instruments transformed into vagabonds, never quite sure where they'll be playing next. I'm not happy with the card, and I've talked about some replacement ideas with Steve, but I think maybe I'll just send it to John and see what he can do with it.

Again.

It's the *Munchkin* way: If it ain't Baroque, don't fix it.[21] ✳

Andrew Hackard is the *Munchkin* czar at Steve Jackson Games. He was also the SJ Games managing editor in a previous lifetime. Andrew has also worked as a math and Latin teacher (not simultaneously), an editor and project manager in educational publishing, and is currently dabbling in professional lassitude and ennui. When not working on *Munchkin*, Andrew can be found curled up on the couch, trying to silence the punsters in his head. It doesn't work. Andrew lives in Round Rock, Texas.

---

[20] Find me at a convention and steer me to the bar, however. . . .
[21] No shame at *all*.

INVOKE EVEN MORE OBSCURE RULES

While standing on one foot, go up two levels, choose another player to go down one level, then draw two Treasure cards and one Door card.

MONTY HAUL AND HIS FRIENDS AT PLAY

David M. Ewalt

I was 10 years old when I tried my first roleplaying game – too young, perhaps, to understand the nuances of a game as complex as *Advanced Dungeons & Dragons*. But what I lacked in maturity, I made up for with intellectual arrogance. I threw myself into the pastime, and within months of discovering it, considered myself an expert. I knew all the rulebooks by heart and could twist them to my will; any time a game master dared to tell me what my character could or could not do, I'd slap him down with a perfectly quoted rule or some obscure bit of arcana. I thought *I* was the master, and I had a pile of badass, high-level characters to prove it.

I still have all of my character sheets from those days, carefully preserved and carried from home to home over three decades, as a jock might hang onto his favorite cleats or lucky baseball bat. But when I look at them now, I don't see evidence of game mastery. Consider "Sir Howland, The Wolf Knight," a 15th-level ranger: Nearly all his ability scores are maxed, he wears +4 plate armor, carries a +4 shield, and is armed with a +6 vorpal sword, a +4 dagger, and a +5 lance. His special abilities are listed on one corner of the sheet in my messy adolescent handwriting: *Incredible senses, great speed, immune to disease, detect evil, summon ethereal sword, black belt in karate and ninjitsu, use technology, time/dimension travel.*

My name is David, and I am a recovering munchkin.

I refer, of course, not to the short-of-stature citizens of Oz in L. Frank Baum's 1900 novel, nor (yet) to the Steve Jackson card game of a century later. I was a munchkin of the mid-1980s variety: a kid who turned a friendly, cooperative roleplaying game into a scramble to exploit the rules, get the most loot, and become the most powerful player at the table – whether or not anyone else had any fun.

The first use of *munchkin* in this pejorative context probably didn't occur during a session of *D&D*, but in one of the historical wargames that gave birth to fantasy roleplaying. Wargames evolved out of board-games like chess, over time becoming increasingly complex simulations of battle. Instead of a king, a queen, and a couple of knights, each player might have hundreds of pieces on the table, ranging from halberdiers to cavalry to cannons. These games were played both as competitive entertainment and as a violence-free simulator of real blood-and-guts war. In the 1860s, the German statesman Otto von Bismarck made a wargame called *Kriegsspiel* part of the standard training regimen for military officers, and historians still cite the game as a contributing factor in decades of Prussian Army victories.

Wargames made their way to the United States in the early

20th century, often carried in the packs of veterans of the two world wars. For decades, the fan base for *Kriegsspiel* and its kin was dominated by men who called themselves "grognards" – a French term for old soldiers. They were a proudly erudite and often crusty lot, obsessed with the minutiae of their favorite game's rules and with military history.

When a group of grognards sat down at the game table, the goal was to accurately simulate real-world battles; creativity was often frowned upon, and fun was welcome but not required.

It's no surprise, then, that some members of the community bristled when their pastime began to go mainstream. In 1952, an Army veteran named Charles S. Roberts created a game called *Tactics* that simplified complex historical wargames such as *Kriegsspiel* into a mass-market boardgame. He followed it up in 1958 with an equally accessible Civil War simulation called *Gettysburg*, and by 1962 Roberts' Avalon Hill Game Company was one of the biggest boardgame publishers in the United States.

Tactics and *Gettysburg* introduced a new type of game to children around the country, and that meant the traditionally gray-haired ranks of local wargaming clubs began to fill up with new, younger members. The crustier grognards began to refer to these upstart players as "munchkins" – a mild slight meant to indicate a young, inexperienced player.

The tension between new and old gamers intensified in the early 1970s, when the munchkins started moving wargaming away from its traditional historical roots. Young, mostly college-aged players introduced elements of fantasy to their simulations, like druid priests using magic to fight Roman armies, instead of swords and spears. Soon they began to play as individual warriors, instead of controlling entire armies – and fantasy roleplaying was born.

The first and most famous of these fantasy roleplaying games (RPGs) was TSR Hobbies' *Dungeons & Dragons*, but there were many others. All of them appealed to gamers because they encouraged creativity and allowed the participants to build vivid imaginary characters and fantasy worlds. But they were still based on rules, and that opened the door for a certain kind of person to subvert the games' intent.

Sometimes the problem was the players – usually young munchkins like me, who focused on exploiting the rules and making their

characters more powerful. At other times, it was the fault of the person running the game – inexperienced game masters who made things too easy for their players, buying their affection with constant rewards of gold, magic items, and experience. These incompetent authorities soon earned their own derogatory nickname; they were "Monty Haul" referees, a reference to Monty Hall, the famously generous host of the TV game show *Let's Make a Deal*.

At first, RPG designers tried to combat the munchkins by adding more rules to their games, in the hopes that no one would be able to keep track of and exploit them all. In the foreword of *Eldritch Wizardry*, a *D&D* supplement published in 1976, editor Tim Kask wrote that the book "should go a long way towards putting back in some of the mystery, uncertainty and danger . . . no more will some foolhardy adventurer run down into a dungeon, find something and immediately know how it works."

It didn't achieve that goal, of course. So the next *D&D* supplement, *Gods, Demi-Gods & Heroes*, added mythological deities such as Zeus and Osiris to the game, in an attempt to cap the progression of high-level munchkin characters: "Perhaps now some of the 'giveaway' campaigns will look as foolish as they truly are," Kask wrote in the foreword. "When Odin, the All-Father has only 300 hit points, who can take a 44th level Lord seriously?"

The munchkins could, that's who, and their numbers were only increasing.

In July 1977, TSR published the *Dungeons & Dragons Basic Set*, a simplified edition designed for people unfamiliar with wargames. Priced inexpensively and sold in toy stores, the *Basic Set* brought fantasy roleplaying to the masses. That meant more kids in the hobby. When *Advanced Dungeons & Dragons* was introduced later that year, it made the problem worse: *Basic* focused on low-level characters, but *AD&D* was designed for higher-level play. It was comprehensive and complex – like crack for munchkins and Monty Haulers.

In the May 1978 issue of the roleplaying magazine *The Dragon*, game designer James Ward lampooned these problem players in an article titled "Monty Haul and His Friends at Play." It's a short story that imagines a group of gamers who keep one-upping each other with ever-more powerful and ridiculous characters: iron golems, knights who ride platinum dragons, and even Martians armed with radiation rifles.

This behavior – both from players and game designers trying to counter it – is ridiculous, of course, and that's the point of Steve Jackson Games' *Munchkin*. At its heart, the beloved card game is an extended riff on those roleplaying fans who engage in the folly of power gaming, the immature competitors who play only to win. We're in on the joke because these "shrieking geeks" are found across the roleplaying landscape, from *D&D* to *Pathfinder* to *GURPS*. We all know them – and all too frequently we *are* them.

Munchkin skewers the behavior of its eponymous subjects with pinpoint accuracy and razor wit. The "Invoke Obscure Rules" card mocks the favorite battle tactic of every desperate nerd that memorized the source books: "No, he didn't hit me, because the *Wilderness Survival Guide* says characters suffer a minus one penalty to attack at night when the only illumination is moonlight." If that doesn't work, they might resort to a "Convenient Addition Error" on an armor class of 12 with a +1 to dodge: "No, he didn't hit me. He needed a fourteen." When all that fails, these players fall back on the ultimate munchkin tactic: "Whine at the GM."

The monster cards reference classic fantasy roleplaying game creatures, too. The "Floating Nose" mocks the beholder, a giant

levitating eye. The "Gelatinous Octahedron" riffs
on the gelatinous cube, which lurks in dungeons
and dissolves unwary adventurers in its acidic
jelly. And the "Platycore" lampoons part-this-
part-that monsters like the hippogriff, man-
ticore, and owlbear. (Of course, in the age
of Harry Potter, you don't have to be an RPG
geek to get a hippogriff gag; like so many other
fantasy icons, the hybrid horse/eagle has gone
mainstream.)

A *Munchkin* deck can actually double nicely as
a storehouse of roleplaying game history. The "Really
Impressive Title" +3 bonus treasure card hearkens back to the short-
lived phenomenon of experience-based honorifics: in first-edition
AD&D, a third-level druid was an "Initiate of the 1st Circle" and a
sixth-level thief was a "Filcher." One of my favorite cards, the level 8
"Gazebo" monster, references a classic story told by game designer
Richard Aronson about a player he knew who considered every angle
and option before acting, but still missed the point entirely. Aronson's
version of the story goes something like this:

> Eric the paladin was traveling across the estate of a rich lord
> when the game master told him, "You see a well-groomed gar-
> den. In the middle, on a small hill, you see a gazebo."
>
> The word was unfamiliar to Eric, so he decided to proceed
> with caution. He drew his sword and cast the spell Detect Good
> upon the gazebo.
>
> "It's not good, Eric," said the game master. "It's a gazebo."
>
> "I call out to it," Eric said.
>
> "It doesn't say anything. It's a gazebo."
>
> Eric put away his sword, readied his bow, and nocked an
> arrow. "Does the gazebo respond?" he asked. It didn't.

"I shoot it with my bow. What happens?"

The game master sighed. "There is now a gazebo with an arrow sticking out of it."

"Did I wound it?" Eric asked.

"No, Eric! It's a gazebo!"

"But that was a plus-three arrow!"

Unable to damage, intimidate, or in any way harm the strange "beast," Eric eventually decided to run away. But by that time, the frustrated GM had experienced all he could take of the paladin's obtuse behavior.

"It's too late," the GM snarled. "You've awakened the gazebo. It catches you and eats you."

Munchkin succeeds as a game because it is well designed and funny, but it has become a classic because it is so richly steeped in these stories and references. It's the ultimate in-joke, told by two game designers who know and love roleplaying geek culture, because they are roleplaying geeks, too.

Steve Jackson has been writing and publishing roleplaying games since the early days of the hobby, including one of the very first "funny" RPGs, 1984's *Toon*, which was designed by Greg Costikyan and developed by Warren Spector. Players take the roles of cartoon characters and are encouraged to break the rules and subvert the conventions of roleplaying games as much as possible; the players' goal is to make one another laugh.

"Back when I was roleplaying regularly, most, though not all, of my groups enjoyed being silly and poking fun at the conventions of the game," Jackson says. "In my very first continuing roleplaying campaign, one of the characters was a dwarf who mounted a chicken on the end of a long pole and carried it in front of him to lure the slimes down from the ceiling. He had to change the chicken regularly, of course, so he carried a supply with him."

Another Steve Jackson publication, 1986's *Generic Universal Role-Playing System*, or *GURPS*, is a classic system that encourages players to experiment with different settings. There's *GURPS Horror* and *GURPS Espionage* and *GURPS Old West*. This desire to leap genres is characteristic of Jackson's work; we see it again in *Munchkin* expansions such as *Munchkin Cthulhu*, *Munchkin Impossible*, and *The Good, the Bad, and the Munchkin*.

Combine a deep familiarity with gamer culture with a willingness to have fun with its conventions, and it's no mystery why Jackson went on to create a card game like *Munchkin*. "My own taste in humor has always leaned toward parody and absurdity, so the whole *Munchkin* thing just clicked," he says. "It's easier to mock what I know."

Munchkin illustrator John Kovalic has a background in roleplaying games, too. He grew up in England in the 1970s, and during a family trip to London, made a fateful stop at the Games Workshop store on Bolingbroke Road. "They had all these little four-page, photocopied pamphlets about what roleplaying is and how you roleplay," he told me. "I had never seen anything like it before, and it just absolutely set my imagination on fire. So I bought these little books and went back to my school in Somerset and formed a roleplaying group, just as thousands if not millions of kids have done since."

The young gamer went on to become a professional cartoonist, and when Steve Jackson asked him to illustrate *Munchkin*, he jumped at the opportunity. "I was just thrilled, absolutely beside myself, because I had been playing Steve's games since the late 1970s," he says. The subject matter resonated with Kovalic, too: "I was very familiar with the kind of game *Munchkin* was describing," he says. "I have had most of those things happen to me in my own gaming sessions."

Kovalic notes that some of his favorite *Munchkin* cards aren't the ones with the most obscure roleplaying game references, but the ones where he's still proud of the illustration – like the "Duck of Doom" and "Spiky Knees." And as much as I revel in RPG arcana, I tend to agree with him. My top cards are the ones that boast great drawings, like "Chicken on Your Head" and "Net Troll," and the corniest jokes, like "Broad Sword," "Pukachu," and "Wight Brothers."

Still, I do love it when a card describes something so familiar it seems ripped straight out of my most recent tabletop roleplaying session. And I love that those references aren't as hard to understand as they used to be. Like Harry Potter and his hippogriff, the RPG nerd is flying high: video games are a $70 billion global business, *The Lord of the Rings* is the highest-grossing film trilogy in history, and they play *D&D* on prime-time network TV. When *Community* and *The Big Bang Theory* can build entire episodes around fantasy RPGs, you know they've gone mainstream.

That's good news for those of us who love roleplaying games. As the pastime enters its fifth decade, the future looks bright; with more people sharing our interests than ever, we may well be entering a golden age for fantasy gaming. Who knows what great games we'll play?

We'll dream of new adventures, of brave heroes that overcome great odds to save the day . . . of treasure and magic items, of piles of gold and silver . . . of great fame and greater power . . . of destroying our enemies and conquering their land . . . of ruling with an iron fist, becoming stronger and stronger – stronger than anyone who has ever lived, until we conquer death itself and travel all the planes of existence . . . of dethroning the gods themselves, and standing triumphant at the center of all of creation, of becoming the ultimate power, the beginning and the end. . . .

Or maybe that's just me. Once a munchkin, always a munchkin. ✳

David M. Ewalt is an award-winning journalist and an authority on the intersection of games and technology. He is the author of the book *Of Dice and Men: The Story of Dungeons & Dragons and The People Who Play It*, which chronicles the history of *D&D*'s origins and the game's impact on business and culture. Find out more at davidmewalt.com.

MONSTER UNION

The monsters have had enough. Each player may add up to two monsters from their hand into the current combat.

MONSTER GRIEVANCES

Jennifer Steen

LETTER TO THE MUNCHKINS 1:

To the Adventurers,

We, the denizens who dwell in your local dungeon, have formed a union to decide all dungeon business. Mostly, though, we have banded together in this way to stop the likes of you from ruining our day. The adventurers that continually tromp into our home are destructive and downright immature. By staying underground like this, away from the cities and villages, we are trying to live in peace. We enjoy spending our time playing games, taking naps, and just being monsters. We have every right to expect freedom from harassment by wizards and elves and assassins!

Yet time after time adventurers show up to kick down our doors, loot our rooms, and engage in destructive behavior, like throwing potions that stick to the walls (and never come off). It's enough to make some of our more sensitive neighbors cry. Countless times, dwarves with outrageously huge axes and eleven-foot poles come bounding through broken doors hacking everything to bits. We have to clean up these messes every time, and we're tired of using tweezers to get the splinters out of our feet and toothbrushes to try and get the potions off the wall.

You – yes, you, adventurer, reading this letter – have been ruining our homestead with your greed for years. We are finally airing our grievances now in hopes of inspiring change. Obviously, we need to educate you on what it's like to be a monster in our dungeon. To this end, let us list some of your most egregious violations:

1. **Disturbance of the Peace.** The dwarves are extremely loud when they splinter the doors, and the rambunctious chanting as they run down the halls doesn't help. Many of us take naps during the day. And then there are the ducks. Let's be clear: we are done with you picking up the ducks – their loud and panicked quacking wakes us at all hours, and it takes forever to quiet the fowl noise. Bigfoot, in particular, is very annoyed because he needs his beauty sleep. We request that any acquired ducks be removed from the dungeon and taken with you. Then you'll truly know our pain and sleepless nights.

2. **Violation of Personal Space.** This applies to all of us, really, but one monster in particular has requested that you do not sit in him. The Gazebo is a sentient being. He is not a place to hang out to watch oompah band concerts or to reenact scenes from *The Sound of Music*. (It's a particularly bad idea to sing "Do-Re-Mi" near him.) He had a bad experience when two lovers were whirling and twirling around him and the girl twirled right through his spindles. His name is Jeremy, and he's a very nice monster once you get to know him. He just has personal space issues and does not like to be touched without asking. Imagine someone sitting in your lap or, worse, your mouth without so much as a hello.

3. **Insult to Injury.** When you come traipsing through our halls, some of you tend to point out our flaws. Not all of us can be tier 1 monsters with names that

unnerve even the bravest adventurer. The Net Troll is quite upset at those of you who kick down his door and make fun of him. Just because he doesn't possess any special powers doesn't mean he can't post an anonymous nasty note about you on Internet message boards. And he thinks he has good cause to do just that. He's angry that you don't understand him. Perhaps you could try to see it from his point of view instead of berating him all the time, especially after you've just bashed him with one of those eleven-foot poles.

4. **Inappropriate Use of Dragons.**  It has come to our attention that some of the adventurers are forcing cute little dragons to sit on their shoulders. Dragons are monsters. They do not belong on your shoulder. While they sometimes *eat* adventurers, most dragons enjoy flying around and sitting on their treasure. We suggest you leave them in the dungeon where dragons belong, and we will take care of them for you. Doing otherwise can only end badly for all those involved. Remember, even little dragons can sometimes breathe fire.

5. **Iä! Iä!** Last, but not least, our comrade, the great and mighty Cthulhu, would like to say a few words. To be specific: *"Dfn'ajt hghw'klk esom'wa rtyawn si rt anna'oj."* We think this means that you should perish in the endless void, but it's always hard to figure out just what he's saying through all those tentacles. He's probably upset because he is having bad dreams, thanks to all the stomping about and fighting going on here. He used to have happy dreams of fluffy bunnies and singing flowers, but now you don't want to know what the dream bunnies look like or what happened to the

singing flowers. You might want to bypass his dungeon door for a while.

To restate our central point: it is difficult to be a monster and hold down a dungeon in this day and age. We hope you understand where we are coming from, or at least can try to act more civilized. Don't you want to be more civilized instead of stubborn, obnoxious, and immature – well, for lack of a better word – munchkins? We hope you'll be willing to work with us. It probably won't take much on your part to make it possible for us all to live in harmony. We eagerly await your reply by dungeon post.

Sincerely,

Monster Union 3872

LETTER TO THE MUNCHKINS 2:

M*unchkins,*

We apologize for using the term *adventurer* to address you instead of *munchkin*, which we have always considered kind of

demeaning and a put-down. In fact, not every one of us likes being called *monster*. We are individuals with feelings and names, too, like Toby the Gummi Golem and Zeddicus the Gothyanki. But you know what you want to be called, no matter the connotations attached to the word by others. From now on we shall call you munchkins.

We are also sorry for the late reply. We were busy with a game of Hide and Go Seek when you last came barreling through our dungeon. While we did not enjoy the fact you destroyed half of our rooms using the Freezing Explosive Potion, we are still laughing at your failure to act as a group.

Once you got inside you were bickering so much with each other that you missed the second entrance to your right. Instead, you all walked right to the edge of the balcony and fell down into the River of Doom. We call this the River Room. It's probably the biggest room in the dungeon and home to the Yak Yak Yaks. They weren't too happy that you got them all wet when you splashed into the river. It takes forever for them to dry off, and we have to spend hours brushing their hair while they talk and talk and talk. They did find it hilarious that you had to run away because all your weapons and shiny armor washed down the river. They've collected all your precious gear and gold to resell to help fix the front door. You might be able to buy it back from the local pawn shop – at a significantly inflated price, of course.

We had mentioned in our previous letter that you should not pick up the ducks. Of course that was the first thing the Dwarf Thief did, and he did it repeatedly. The noise was absolutely horrific. How could he not notice that the ducks kept getting louder every time he picked one up? It's not just about the noise; it's the lack of respect these actions show for our personal space. Please stop doing this!

Also, your Hirelings thought it would be a great idea to take a selfie with every monster without asking. We are not responsible for what happened after the camera flash went off.

We understand that some of you munchkins were having difficulty figuring out the meaning of our first letter. In the simplest terms, we, the monsters of Union 3872, would like to propose a truce. To show our sincerity, we want you to know that we have something precious of yours. You may not be able to figure out what it is but we are holding it for ransom. It might take you a while to figure out which treasure is gone; trust us when we say you'll miss it. Below is a map showing a location where you can meet us to discuss the truce. We hope you are amenable to this proposal.

Sincerely,

Monster Union 3872

LETTER TO THE MUNCHKINS 3:

Munchkins,

We have had it up to here with your selfishness. You didn't show up for our proposed meeting. Instead, you have shown complete disregard for us by entering our dungeon and stealing more of our treasure. This is the second time in two days that you have blasted our front door into pieces. (Squidzilla had just put the finishing touches to a final coat of brown paint on the new door, too.) And why even enter that way? Did you even read the map we included in the last letter? If you had, you would have realized that there are a dozen less destructive places to enter the dungeon. Really, give the map a look. Get your friends to help you. Perhaps one who knows which side of the map is north.

We really wanted to settle our mutual grievances like civilized monsters and munchkins. We believed you could handle that kind of discussion, but perhaps we were wrong. This letter may come off as a bit more ominous, but we are trying to make a point. We were going to make amends and return your property to you, but now we won't unless you start being nice. Hopefully by now you have figured out that we have your precious *Munchkinomicon*. Don't worry about how we ended up with your spellbook. We have it. Let's move on.

The book is being safeguarded by the most ferocious of beasts, one you may have never before encountered. If you want to have the *Munchkinomicon* back, send a designated representative to the darkest part of the dungeon to sign our truce. If you are thinking of using the truce meeting as a cover for you to attack our home elsewhere, we'll only note that the dungeon is boasting some new traps. Psycho Squirrel and the Hippogriff haven't been happy with what's been going on. They've spread some really nasty stuff around, such as buckets of sticky purple paint. The squirrels have used some of that potion that changes the size of an item to create boulder-sized nuts. Also, the Plutonium Dragon really outdid himself this time.

Attached is a new map of where you can find your precious book. Being munchkins and all, you'll need all the help you can get, so we've made the map really simple. We will be awaiting your arrival. Remember: *do not* pick up any ducks you encounter along the way.

Annoyed,

Monster Union 3872

LETTER TO THE MUNCHKINS 4:

Munchkins,

    We are deeply saddened – and, frankly, infuriated – by your inability to understand what it means to attend a meeting. We hoped you could follow our directions from the previous letters and conclude our dealings in a positive fashion. Once again you decided to raid, and you continue to pick up the ducks. We have to conclude now that you are doing this out of spite. Regardless, your behavior has had dire repercussions. Some of the ducks have taken to dyeing their feathers black and moping around like the sun will never shine again. We can't make these gloomy ducks happy, and those that remain yellow simply act out all day. This is just one of the more obvious ways in which you've made a mess of our dungeon.

We found our three previous letters crumpled up in the bottom of a sack that was dropped by a fleeing munchkin. It's utterly appalling that you would treat the letters like trash, particularly after we spent hours making certain the penmanship they displayed was perfect. We have to wonder now if you even read the letters, or if you simply don't care about their message. Either way, based on your utter lack of respect, we are taking extraordinary measures.

We're going to let you in on a little secret. By now you've probably gone through your loot that you stole from the dungeon last night and are cheering that you got your *Munchkinomicon* back.

Before you entered the dungeon, we, as a union, decided that if you weren't going to be amenable to a truce, we'd have to do something drastic to keep you out of our home. To this end, we created a new book identical to the one you used to possess. Then, while you were looting the rooms, the Poison Ivy Kudzu Flytrap hid the book in Fredrick the Bard's burlap sack.

Some denizens suggested putting a curse on the book that would make you paranoid so that you would constantly squabble amongst yourselves and sacrifice your treasure. But the dragons sagely noted that you already act like this. Instead, the curse we ended up placing on the book will make you cooperate with each other and suffer from guilty consciences when screwing each other over. You will be so busy being racked by guilt that we should finally enjoy some peace and quiet around here.

All we really wanted to do was come to an understanding, and we're sorry (well, some of us, anyway) that this is how things turned out. Good luck if you try to get back into the dungeon. Take that as a final warning. But just in case that doesn't work, let's be clear: we're done playing nice. Bring it on.

Defiantly,

Monster Union 3872 ✴

Jennifer Steen hosts the ENnie-nominated *Jennisodes* podcast, where she poses hard-hitting interview questions to a myriad of individuals in the gaming community. She has conversed with game designers, authors, editors, artists, and players of all sorts over the past three years. She is also the designer of the zany and outrageously fun story-telling RPG, *Project Ninja Panda Taco*. When she isn't taking over the world through podcasting and reining in minions, she enjoys playing *Magic: The Gathering*, eating tacos, and wishing she had a panda. She lives in Philadelphia, PA, and is often found playing games with her wonderful husband, baby munchkin, and two monsterlike puppies.

MILLION-POUND EXPLETIVE HAMMER

This is a 2-handed Big item that gives a +4 bonus to start. Each time someone curses, either verbally or by playing a Curse card on someone else in the game, the Million-Pound Expletive Hammer gets a permanent +1. This card cannot be lost to Curses – it smashes them to bits. If lost to Bad Stuff or to Death, feel free to curse, as it's gone forever.

SCREW YOU, PRETTY
BALLOONS

THE COMEDY OF MUNCHKIN

Joseph Scrimshaw

T he famous German philosopher Hegel declared, "Comedy is negation!"

To which the majority of other comic theorists replied, "No, it's not."

I believe all great comedy philosophers would agree *Munchkin* is a very funny game. In fact, I risk no hyperbole when I say *Munchkin* is one of the funniest of the three games I own. (The other games are *Monopoly* and *Star Wars Monopoly*.)

Obviously, I don't own a lot of games, and I deeply regret that I wasted my early twenties getting an expensive liberal arts degree when I should have been buckling down and really playing the hell out of *Dungeons & Dragons*.

The one class I took in college that truly stuck with me was called Introduction to Comic Theory. Ever since I took that class, I've been hoarding laugh treasure, killing audience monsters, and leveling up as a writer and performer of comedy.

My professor (or comedy Dungeon Master) for Introduction to Comic Theory had a great phrase that would make an even better *Munchkin* card. He described the act of studying comedy as cracking open jokes by hitting them with a Million-Pound Expletive Hammer. He didn't say "expletive," because this was a liberal arts class, and anything goes, man. But you get the point.

This essay poses such questions as: Why is *Munchkin* so funny? Why does it want to be funny? Doesn't *Munchkin* want to be taken seriously? Doesn't it want to win dramatic awards like *The Wire* edition of *Monopoly* probably does?

Some, if not all, of these questions will be answered using the time-tested comic theories of philosophers such as Sigmund Freud, Henri Bergson, and some guy named Scrimshaw who openly admits to owning *Star Wars Monopoly*.

In other words, it's time to whip out our Million-Pound Expletive Hammers and bang the expletive out of that damn funny game called *Munchkin*.

CONTRAST

Most comic philosophers agree that all comedy functions on contrast. Human beings are wired to laugh at two incongruous ideas smashed together. If you want to test this theory, go tell a three-year-old that the sound a duck makes is "moo."

Most children will find this hilarious. Overly serious children will become violently angry that you would waste their time with this nonsense, then stomp off to watch *The Wire*. Either way, the comedy magic happens.

The comedy of *Munchkin*'s basic premise functions on contrast. The highest goals of *Dungeons & Dragons* – slowly building the narrative reality of your characters, carefully monitoring your dwarf's hit points, spinning a grand tale of adventure – are smashed into the

more honest goals proudly emblazoned
on the front cover of *Munchkin*: Kill
the monsters, steal the treasure,
stab your buddy.

This also gives us our first peek
into the purpose of comedy: catharsis. One of the many ways comedy provides pleasurable emotional release is
by allowing us to express an otherwise difficult truth in a socially
acceptable manner.

In this example, *Munchkin* allows
us to say, "Okay, fine, you got me. I don't care about my elf's backstory
or motivation. I don't give a damn about the history of the forest we're
walking through. I just want to stab this stupid wizard in his stupid
back and take his stupid wand because it will make me feel awesome."
In other words, the game lets us be honest that even when playing a
potentially complex, sophisticated game such as *Dungeons & Dragons*,
all humans take at least a little bit of glee in greed, mayhem, and feeling as powerful and potent as possible.

To research this essay, I set up a sample game of *Munchkin* with
as much comic contrast as possible. I played a game with the following players:

My wife, Sara. Sara and I don't own a lot of games, but we frequently
play tabletop games with friends. Sara has alternately enjoyed and
tolerated many hours of me relating the details of a *Call of Cthulhu*
campaign. She is not particularly well versed in *D&D* lore, but she
spends enough time at SF/fantasy conventions to be familiar with
the basics.

Our friends, Jim and Dennis. Jim and Dennis are partners. Dennis
is a lifelong gamer and, at the time of this writing, is in the middle of

DMing an ongoing fourth-edition *Dungeons & Dragons* campaign. Jim, on the other hand, has never played *Dungeons & Dragons*. In fact, he admits to frequently forgetting the name of the game and referring to it as *Bats & Basements*. Jim is also a professor of abnormal psychology who loves Carly Simon and ennui.

Before we even started to play, Jim looked at the really rather small *Munchkin* rules pamphlet and said, "Oh, so many rules."

Dennis asked, "So, this essay will be about theories of comedy?"

Jim then noted, "I fell down on the ice in front of a child yesterday. Maybe you could write about that. I mean, it's such a ridiculous feeling to fall down as an adult. You're standing upright and proper and then you start flailing around like an idiot. You know you're falling and there's nothing you can do to stop it."

"That's kind of what's going to happen in this game," I said.

"I also swore in front of a child while I was falling."

"Swearing will happen, too," said Dennis.

And so we began to play.

THE JOKING ENVELOPE

Before play begins in a violently funny game such as *Munchkin*, all combatants must first step inside Sigmund Freud's joking envelope.

This is not as creepy as it sounds.

In Sigmund Freud's book on comic theory, *Jokes and Their Relation to the Unconscious*, the term *joking envelope* refers to the idea that comedy is a form of packaging for ideas and emotions. In a larger sense, the term has come to express the social space in which we agree any idea has the potential for comedy.

Within the safe confines of the joking envelope, we accept that malicious or cruel statements are intended as humor.

For example, saying, "I am going to steal everything you own, you expletive-hat!" is a pretty friendly, run-of-the-mill thing to say while playing *Munchkin*.

It's probably not something you want to say to the server when you walk into Chipotle to order a burrito.

Your friends at the *Munchkin* table are inside the joking envelope. The server at Chipotle is not.

The social protection of the joking envelope also extends to actions. Many *Munchkin* players don't waste their time with petty verbal taunts. Instead they follow that age-old wisdom, "Talk softly and carry an Eleven-Foot Pole." Then they direct their munchkins to beat their friends' characters silly with it, because, of course, a large portion of the comedy inherent to *Munchkin* is in the screw-over-your-friends mechanics.

In a typical game of *Munchkin*, it's hard to accomplish even the simplest task – say, defeating a Potted Plant with an axe – because your friends are so anxious to screw you over.

Subsequently, a player might shout out something like, "Dammit! I can't accomplish even the simplest little task!"

This honest statement will be met with gales of laughter from the friends and loved ones gathered around the table with you.

Imagine the same scenario at your typical office job. All you want to do is turn your computer on so you can log in and start getting paid. Your friend walks up and unplugs the computer. You plug it back in, and you wait for it to start up. You reach for your keyboard and mouse. Your spouse shows up at your place of employment, rips the mouse out of your hand, throws it out the window, takes five dollars out of your wallet, and laughs at you.

"*Why?*" you would scream. "Why won't you let me accomplish even the simplest little task?"

(I offer the above scenario to Steve Jackson Games to use, free of charge, should they ever want to release *Munchkin Real Life Office Horror*.)

Strangely, our game of *Munchkin* featured little to no friend-hosing horror.

Instead, in another example of comic contrast, my sample game of *Munchkin* proved to be shockingly friendly. Here are some of the great burns we shouted at one another:

"I'm sorry!"

"Was that okay?"

"I didn't realize that would make you lose your Eleven-Foot Pole!"

"I keep hurting people when I don't mean to!"

Eventually, the tide turned as Dennis, the experienced gamer, started to bring the hammer down. He pointed out to the other players that I was winning. "Stop being nice!" Dennis shouted. "This guy is on level eight! He is Mister Expletive Threat Prime!"

All laughed and nodded in agreement. It was true. I was Mister Expletive Threat Prime. I was not offended at being called this because I was inside the joking envelope.

I joined in the laughter because calling people names and screwing them over is fun.

Besides, a joke is just a joke, right?

In the bastardized words of Sigmund Freud, "Sometimes an Amazon with a Magic Missile is just an Amazon with a Magic Missile."

And sometimes, it's a great big, adult humor-type joke.

INNOCENT VERSUS
TENDENTIOUS HUMOR

Freud's *Jokes and Their Relation to the Unconscious* also argues that there are two distinct forms of humor: innocent and tendentious.

Innocent humor is simple word play – odd, surprising, amusing contrasts that are not trying to make a point or reveal a larger truth, but simply amuse with their light absurdity.

Individual *Munchkin* cards are great examples of innocent word play. The card "Broad Sword" gives the player a sword that can only be used by a woman, thus making a light, safe funny by contrasting the two meanings of the word *broad*.

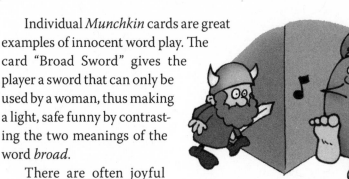

There are often joyful visual jokes in John Kovalic's artwork, too. On the card "Wandering Monster" from the first *Munchkin* set, the monster has a spacey look on his face and is casually whistling, while the brave Warrior seems consumed with fear. It's a simple, effective, and hilarious contrast. We really don't think of monsters whistling as they happily bounce down the dungeon corridors.

Our gameplay featured plenty of innocent humor. For added theatricality, I asked the other players to narrate their defeat of monsters with some fun action noises. Sara bested a level 10 Floating Nose with her third-level Elf Cleric, then made copious sniffing noises.

It was funny because my wife doesn't usually make big honking, snorting noises at our dinner table.

She also added, "I was sniffling because it's a nose." This was more great innocent comedy, because, like, we knew that. Still, we all laughed.

Then, the darkness came again. Jim drew a door card. We all commented, "Wow! No monster in the room."

Jim sighed and said, "The monster was me all along."

Freud's other comedy category – tendentious humor – is far more prevalent and potent. Tendentious comedy is any joke that has meaning; it's a joke that is meant to expose some truth or cause cathartic laughter by saying something grossly inappropriate within the safety of the joking envelope. For example, a quip that really means:

"I, Jim, as a simple human man, am a far worse monster than any I could find in a dungeon."

Munchkin offers plenty of humor of the tendentious sort. Dennis, the *D&D* veteran, drew a card, roared with laughter, and said out loud, "Oh, that is funny."

He then showed us all the "Lawyer" card. He was even more amused to see that the "Insurance Salesman" was such a high-level monster.

In a modern cultural context, calling a lawyer a monster isn't too shocking, but it's a perfect example of Freud's classification of tendentious humor. It is not word play and it is not innocent. It's a clear statement: Lawyers are just as evil, if not more, as a vampire, a ghoul, or – depending on which version of *Munchkin* you are playing – the unfathomable menace of Cthulhu himself.

For such cards to have their full effect, the audience has to get the complex intent and sort out the meanings pretty quickly. For some *Munchkin* cards, that also means possessing a solid knowledge of gamer culture. Dennis, for example, played the card "Bribe GM With Food."

Dennis and I laughed.

Jim stared.

Dennis explained, "The GM is the game master. He's the guy who runs roleplaying games like *Dungeons & Dragons*. The kind of game *Munchkin* is satirizing."

"It's a stereotype that a lot of gamers eat a lot of really crappy food while gaming," I added.

SCREW YOU, PRETTY BALLOONS

"Is it true?" Jim asked.

Dennis and I nodded in a sage, meaningful, tendentious manner.

But tendentious humor is not just jokes that make a statement. They are also jokes that express indecent, uncomfortable, or potentially offensive ideas. A few *Munchkin* cards that gleefully wander into this dark side of the comedy dungeon include "Crabs," "Pukachu," and "Stoned Golem."

A few turns after bribing the GM with food, I asked Jim to please make the combat noises when he defeated a monster with his Magic Missile.

Jim responded with a series of small groans, then explained, "That's a little adult humor." And we all laughed.

Because in tendentious comedy, a Magic Missile is always a great big, absurd, magical adult humor joke.

After Jim had destroyed an Undead Horse with a Magic Missile (and adult humor), it was once again my turn. I was very close to victory.

Until my wife screwed me over – and everyone laughed.

Why? Why was it so funny to have the joy crushed out of me?

As always with such deep, philosophical matters, the French have an opinion on this.

ENCRUSTATION OF THE MECHANICAL ON THE LIVING VERSUS *ÉLAN VITAL*

The French philosopher Henri Bergson argues that all comedy arises specifically from the contrast between what he describes as encrustation of the mechanical on the living versus *élan vital.*

Élan vital, roughly translated as "the vital force," refers to the inner spirit of humanity that makes one feel alive. Encrustation of the mechanical on the living reflects anything that holds that spirit back – repetitive ideas, repetitive chores, the repetitive beat of daily life, and, in a modern sense, the repetitive drone of technology.

Perhaps the greatest example of this weird French theory is autocorrect. Your human spirit wants to communicate the simple message to your mother, "I'm in line at Chipotle!" However, your iPhone encrusts your *élan vital* and insists on telling your mother that you are "in licking a chandelier."

The simple comedy of contrast is at work here, but Bergson argues it goes deeper. He postulates that the more our pure human desires are crushed by an external, mechanical system, the more hilarity ensues.

If Bergson were still alive, he would immediately die laughing at *Munchkin*.

In the rules, this very funny joke is made more than once. One of the best examples is: if you don't have a class card, you have no class.

Jim found this funny. He kept dryly saying to anyone who didn't have a class card, "You have no class."

For our game, it became Jim's own little catchphrase.

Bergson would argue that catchphrase humor is another example of encrustation. Most catchphrases start out as actual funny jokes or incidents bursting with *élan vital*.

Repeated once, it's a callback. Repeated a third time, it completes the arbitrary comedy "rule of three."

But comedy (and humans playing tabletop games) love to break their own rules, so we keep repeating the same jokes until they are encrusted and unfunny. By the eighth time Jim said, "You have no class," it was once again hilarious because it really shouldn't be funny anymore and thus successfully recreated contrast.

Catchphrases that are shared across a large community – like the *Munchkin* cry of "Duck of Doom!" – collect meaning over time.

Eventually, their humor functions on the basic contrast between the simplicity of the original statement and the ridiculous complexity of its history.

If you're at a Star Wars convention and you shout "Han shot first!" everyone in attendance could write a 10,000-word essay on the history and meaning of that statement. If you walk back into that Chipotle you've already been kicked out of once today for saying something weird, and shout "Han shot first!" they will think you have aphasia.

Catchphrases are also funny because they often distract you from your main point, so let's get back to Bergson.

In a larger sense, in the game of *Munchkin*, all we want to do is what it says on the front of the box: Kill, steal, and stab. All we want to do is follow our pure human desire to destroy monsters and become the most powerful person at the dining room table.

But the very game that allows us to pursue these fantasies of power also has a thousand obnoxious ways to screw us out of seeing them fulfilled.

For the last several rounds of our sample game, I was a level 9 Human Thief with a Huge Rock. I should have been all-powerful, but no! My loved ones found great comic joy in playing card after card to impede my glorious victory: "Curse!" "Out to Lunch," "Steal a Level," "+10 to Monster," and even "Pretty Balloons."

My deep, instinctual human longing for power was crushed by Pretty Balloons.

Of course, in the moment, I didn't find it that funny.

Some might explain this by turning to Woody Allen's quote of a famous line in *Crimes and Misdemeanors*: "Comedy is tragedy plus time."

I say bull-*expletive*, Mister Allen, because my friends and wife thought my tragedy was pretty funny at the time.

In fact, I would argue that the joy of comedy is always immediate.

GRIMSHANK'S PARADIGM

My final comic theory is one that I pompously coined myself. If life were a *Munchkin* game, this theory would have been created by drawing the "Pull a Theory Out of Your Hat" card.

Grimshank's Paradigm is this: Comedy repeats on itself.

This is not a fart joke, but it could be if you want to interpret it that way. I can't control your thoughts. *Yet.*

Comedy functions on violence. It happens when expectations are broken and when contrasting ideas are smashed together. Successful comedy causes an explosion of laughter. In *Munchkin*, screwing over your friends kills them twice over: it elicits raucous laughter while allowing you to actually murder their characters.

Even though comedy functions through metaphorical violence, its purpose is pure, honest joy. When we cruelly laugh at our friend's impotent attempts to defeat a Potted Plant, we are in that very same moment creating the joy of catharsis.

Munchkin, in particular, allows us to poke fun of ourselves as gamers. It helps us laugh at the instincts toward greed and power that we all share as flawed, classless level 1 Humans. When we steal certain triumph out of the hands of our loved ones, we aren't just screwing them over, we're also giving them the gift of laughter.

Comedy turns what should be petty and cruel into something beautiful.

That should be the end of the story. But comedy exists to poke fun at things like overly serious endings, so the cycle continues.

Grimshank's Paradigm argues that comedy is a relentless, unstoppable monster that you can't run away from, no matter what. Even when it allows us to reach the noble heights of healthy catharsis, it can't resist the opportunity to make a smart-ass comment about the situation.

As a comedian, it's tempting to obey the monstrous spirit of

comedy – to create joy through mocking, then turn around and mock that joy.

In practice, however, it's best to try to make your point, get a laugh, and leave your audience wanting more.

So it was in my sample game of *Munchkin*. I don't win games very often. I thought it would be pretty awesome if I legitimately won this game, so I could write about it in an essay.

And I did.

I, Joseph Scrimshaw, a level 9 Human Thief, used a Huge Rock to crush a level 1 Lame Goblin.

I beamed with manly pride.

Then my good friend Dennis said, "I only let you win so you can say you did in your stupid comedy essay."

We all laughed. We laughed much, much harder than if we had just played stupid old *Star Wars Monopoly*.

Thanks, *Munchkin*. Thanks, restless spirit of comedy. Thanks, friends.

And screw you, Pretty Balloons. ✳

Joseph Scrimshaw is a comedian, writer, and squirrel enthusiast based in Los Angeles. He's brought his geek-flavored comedy to the San Francisco SketchFest, Chicago Improv Festival, Jonathan Coulton's JoCo Cruise Crazy, and more. He's written for John Kovalic's Dork Storm Press, *RiffTrax*, the public radio show *Wits*, and James Urbaniak's podcast *Getting On with James Urbaniak*. Joseph's podcast *Obsessed* has been featured as a "Staff Favorite" on iTunes and listed in the top 100 comedy podcasts. Joseph's first book, *Comedy of Doom*, was released in July 2012, and his comedy and music album, *Flaw Fest*, entered the world in November 2013. His hit plays *Adventures in Mating, The Worst Show in the Fringe, An Inconvenient Squirrel,* and *My Monster* (written with Bill Corbett) have been performed all over the world. In his free time, Joseph wastes all his free time tweeting about not having enough free time.

Exact Change Dance!

Use this rule after you have sold *exactly* 1,000 Gold Pieces to go up a level. You must stand up, say, "Exact Change! Wooo!" and do a little dance. You may then go up a *second* level, for free. This may not be the winning level unless you are playing against Randy Scheunemann.

ON WITH THE SHOW

CONFESSIONS OF A MUNCHKIN DEMO PRO

Randy Scheunemann

I play games for a living. There's more to my job than that, but the rest of it is tied up in everything else that publishing games requires. Since 2005, a big part of my time has been spent playing different Steve Jackson Games releases, *Munchkin* foremost among them, and teaching them to people around the world. It has been informative, frustrating, and even liberating.

As it turns out, people love *Munchkin*. Tons of people – millions of people – love *Munchkin*. The game is everywhere these days, in all kinds of stores, from the smallest hobby shop to the largest retail mega-chain. So it's understandable that I sometimes forget there are folks who aren't familiar with it. These are the people who cautiously walk up to our booth at a convention and, after eyeing all the colorful banners and the stacks and stacks of new games, ask, "What is *Munchkin*?" It's always a bit of a shock, that question, but I recover quickly and begin my spiel.

More often than not, the players I introduce to *Munchkin* are newcomers to the world of hobby gaming. This makes me an ambassador of sorts, and demoing a game like *Munchkin* means opening people up to something new. I let them know that boardgaming doesn't have to be about shoes and top hats trying to bankrupt their friends, or players arguing about whether or not *sheeps* is a valid plural of *sheep*, because that extra S would mean a triple word score.

The key to running a good demo is familiarity, knowing a game inside and out, and my time at Steve Jackson Games has certainly made me familiar with *Munchkin*. I've shipped it to people. I've fought through new release days, the madness of the holiday season, and long-awaited reprints. For inventory checks and warehouse moves, I've counted and carted more boxes than I care to remember.

Then there's playtesting. Wow, have I playtested a lot of *Munchkin* sets. For those of you unfamiliar with game design lingo, playtesting is when you get people together to try out a design that's not quite finished. The goal is to find weaknesses, broken rules, or elements that bog down play. When it comes to playtesting, I possess the gift of destruction. More than one *Munchkin* set has a "because of Randy" rule thanks to some flaw in the design I discovered in the playtest.

I have also toured the country promoting *Munchkin*. During those trips I've seen every kind of local game shop imaginable. There are as many different kinds of game shops as there are cities and towns across the globe. Quite a lot of them carry *Munchkin*, though their opinions on what the company can do to help them sell more copies and make their customers happy vary almost as much as the game stores themselves. But I've learned to value every shop owner's opinion. Their perspective on the game helps me expand my own.

I've even worn the *Munchkin* mascot costume. Donning that thing means sweating more than you ever thought possible. Oh, and you have to maneuver with your vision confined to the carpet directly in front of your feet. (There was a

time when I could identify convention venues by their carpet patterns.) On the upside, I've been photographed more often than some movie stars. But all that nonstop attention is tough to take. So much so that I've developed a deep respect for people who spend their daily lives in the public eye, now that I've walked a mile in oversized Boots of Butt-Kicking.

Most importantly, I've demoed *Munchkin*. A lot. I have let people win. I've had novices crush me, and I've passed that pain along to overconfident veterans. It's always a little sad when players can't stick around long enough to finish a game, particularly the ones that have gone in interesting directions. But con-goers are busy folks. They have other places to be or things to do at the convention, so they hurry off, leaving me to wonder how the rest of the contest might have played out. Sometimes the convention floor is so loud that I have to pantomime instructions. Other times, it's quiet enough that you can hear the players' laughter all the way across the hall.

Every single one of those demos, whether a complete game or just a round or two, has helped further my understanding of *Munchkin*.

KNOW YOUR AUDIENCE

Before I delve into the role of conventions and more details on the nuts and bolts of running a demo, let me take a minute to talk about the types of demos I've done over the years. Demoing a game like *Munchkin* is not a one-size-fits-all activity. Audience is everything, and there are several different audiences for any game.

Playing with game designers is not like playing with normal people. (But in a good way, of course.) Because I work at Steve Jackson

Games, I participate in demos that involve men and women who make games for a living. These can be demonstrations for playtest purposes, to gather feedback for a design's revision, or for educational purposes, to give everyone a working familiarity with a new release or a refresher on a classic before convention season. Typically, I know the people gathered around the table for these events far better than I know the game itself. In this case, that's acceptable, as designers tend to want to reference the precise wording of the rules as they play, to make certain they understand the mechanics. Until recently, *Munchkin* was the only game I demoed in-house at SJ Games that I hadn't playtested for its original release. With the new edition of *Ogre* and the reprinting of a few of our older games, such as *Car Wars* and *Knightmare Chess*, that's no longer true.

The people who make up the next audience aren't designers, but they take their gaming just as seriously. These are the thought leaders. They want to learn the game in ways that allow them to talk about it, and perhaps even teach it, to a wider audience. Some are super-fans. They already know about the latest releases and they're at the SJ Games convention booth to give them a try. (The super-fans are often easy to spot. They're the first ones to show up at the booth at any major convention, clad in their *Munchkin* T-shirts, which are, of course, already signed.) Others are stalwarts like the Steve Jackson Games demo team, the storied Men In Black (or MIBs), as well as bloggers, reviewers, and other gaming trendsetters. For this audience we create special Internet videos, stage game-launch events, and even run special seminars so they have everything they need to spread the good word about *Munchkin* far and wide.

Game distributors and store owners share some similarities with thought leaders as a demo audience, but they also have special concerns. They want to know if *Munchkin* is fun and easy to learn, just like any demo audience. They also have to consider a whole raft of other details, everything from the potential appeal of the box cover art to the product's retail and wholesale prices. A successful demo to these folks can mean thousands or even hundreds of thousands of copies of a game making their way to store shelves, but they're typically mulling over new releases from a lot of different companies. Time is at a premium for them, so their demo needs to be fast and efficient.

Last, but certainly not least, are the individuals who might spend their money on a copy of *Munchkin*, whether for themselves or as a gift. A demo to someone from this audience may only sell one copy of the game and that sale might not even occur until days or weeks later, but we still put a lot of effort into it. In fact, these demos are the trickiest to pull off with any consistency, since the participants can be so varied. And as hobby and media conventions continue to attract ever wider audiences, the potential demo participants will only get more diverse.

CONVENTIONS AND CONVERTS

Earlier I mentioned demoing games at conventions. I've had the good fortune to attend some of the largest game, comic book, and media conventions in the world. I can tell you from experience that every convention is different. Each and every one has its own soul, which can't be replicated. My role at each show is a little different, too. Sometimes SJ Games staff sells products to the attendees. Other times we have companies such as Adventure Retail handle sales while we focus on demos. At some shows there are no sales at all; we only run demos and hand out promotional items.

It's hard to say whether I find it more exciting to work at a convention where many of the attendees have never played *Munchkin* before, or one where the vast majority of attendees know our games well. It's great to talk with players familiar with Steve Jackson Games, who want to learn about upcoming releases and share their enthusiasm for our product lines. On the flip side, demoing *Munchkin* with someone unfamiliar with the game means giving them the chance to kick down

that door for the first time and being there to see their smiles after they do.

Either way, the ability to spend time face-to-face with people is what matters. At a convention, I can show potential customers what's inside a box before they buy it. They can see the rulesheet, feel the cards, and even roll the die for free. And if they stick around for a demo, they can play the game itself. If it's not a regular Steve Jackson Games employee guiding them through that experience, chances are it's one of the Men In Black. Members of this elite support team are experts in the games they demo, trained to make your convention experience a great one.

Cons are also a great place to highlight gaming's social aspects. If the people gathered around a demo table are loudly laughing, cheering, or even groaning, new people are going to stop to see what's going on. This plays right into *Munchkin*'s strengths. The game elicits strong reactions from players; one of *Munchkin*'s major design victories is that each card presents a sharp-edged little joke to be enjoyed and shared as it is revealed. The game's heart beats each time a new card is drawn. And since the game's mechanics are easily understood, the onlookers drawn to the cheerful ruckus are often quick to declare, "I've got the next game."

At a show, *Munchkin* veterans are typically quite happy to welcome neophytes to the fold. These longtime fans frequently amaze me. They're the lifeblood of the world I live in. They come from all walks of life and just about every corner of the world. They are everyone and anyone. It can be humbling to meet someone who exhibits an intense passion for a game you've had even the smallest role in publishing, all the more because they're usually quite vocal about their devotion. That's the point of the convention for me – to get the chance to introduce the game to new players, and chat a few minutes here and there with the fans that come to the show, sometimes year after year. They're the first ones to let me know I've been missed if I can't attend a convention for some reason. When we do get a chance to talk, they want the newest news, the newest product, the newest promo – and we love them for it.

A Demo Is Born

The convention or store demo for a new game or game expansion starts life in pretty rough shape, even if the person running the demo has the rules down pat. In theory, you know the system. In theory, you should be able to deal with any questions a player might raise. In theory.

In practice, situations can arise during a demo early in the convention season that the rules don't cover, no matter how carefully they were tested. Demo players, especially novices, have the uncanny knack of playing cards in a way that challenges that one rule that might have been written a little more clearly. It usually takes a few sessions before the most obvious of these problems reveal themselves, and they're solved easily enough. But there's also the question of the demo's optimal number of players, as well as the range of players it can accommodate. Too many people at the table will create lag between each player's turn. Too few and the demo master might have to act as an additional player. I find taking on that extra role diverts my focus from the overall gaming experience and limits the attention I can give each player.

The more sessions of a demo you run, the stronger it gets. In the early going, I tend to feel that a demo is missing something that will only manifest over time. It's kind of like the difference between the first performances of a long-running play and the last. I do everything I can to make early-season demos great, but they just aren't as polished as the ones I run at the end of the year. With practice, the phrasing I need to explain the game succinctly and elegantly rolls off the tongue. Over time, I discover initial setups that convey a lot of information and identify points in the game where a demo can end if time runs short. It's better to play through to the end, but the point of a demo table is to give as many people as possible the chance to give the game a try.

I know I have the demo in peak form when I start hearing my lines repeated by the other staffers or MIBs running the game in our booth. They'll never follow my script to the letter, and that's a good thing. Everyone runs a demo a little differently. As the season wears on, they'll develop their own scripts and pick up bits of other presentations, whatever will help them get the game in front of people and allow them to hit the key sales points.

I'll admit, I used to get slightly annoyed by others deviating from the way I had shown them to run the demo. I had, after all, perfected it, so they had to be offering an inferior version. I soon realized, though, that the presenter's comfort with the script is more important than the script itself. So when someone was adopting only the bits of my "routine" they felt comfortable with, they were really creating a better version of their own demo, not a worse version of mine. I should have been encouraged by the amount of my material they were saving rather than disappointed by the amount that they had discarded.

Once a demo has been streamlined, it takes a lot less mental energy and time to run. A good script anticipates questions about the game, leaving more opportunities for the demo master to engage the players and the onlookers while the session is going on. That, in turn, means more people pass through the booth with good information – and that's the main reason to run demos in the first place.

Beyond the Demo

When I can, I like to follow up a demo with a little gift that will help the players remember what game they just sampled. *Munchkin*, of course, is famous for its promotional items. Cards are some of our most common and popular promo creations, and when they're available, I slip our newest ones into any demo I run. We've done lots of other types of items over the years: T-shirts, coins, bookmarks, even cookies. As with the demos, it's "practice makes perfect" with promotional gimmicks; each new item teaches us valuable lessons about how to make them work more effectively at conventions or trade shows. Some venues, for example, don't appreciate it when you give away water labeled "magic potion" because it cuts into their concession sales. It's also a bad idea to hand out stickers with your company's name on them, because they'll end up stuck all over the place and the maintenance staff will know precisely who to blame.

The occasional small misstep aside, all the little promo items SJ Games releases for *Munchkin* add a wonderful level of chaos and absurdity to the game. In fact, I'd go so far as to say that it's impossible to separate the *Munchkin* promotional and auxiliary items from the game proper. And all you need to know to use them is whatever text comes with the item. If the item is a shirt, wear the shirt and get the bonus. If it's a card, do what the card says. There's even a special rule for this essay and for the book in which this essay appears. As a *Munchkin* player, you get a bonus for reading about getting bonuses with auxiliary items. How fun is that? The most faithful *Munchkin* fans collect these items ardently, and they've been known to bring a smile to the face of even the most casual player who pauses for a quick demo at a show.

Looking ahead, I cannot predict the future of demos. I'm sure that some technological breakthrough will revolutionize the way I do things, adding new methods by which I can connect with players and potential players, but my crystal ball is a bit foggy. I suspect it will have something to do with the massive communication abilities we have at our fingertips every hour of the day. Perhaps we'll get a virtual reality setup where a person could play a demo with me without having to leave home. That seems farfetched and yet realistic at the same time, where *Munchkin* is concerned.

I hope to have a place in the process no matter what the future holds, and I know that *Munchkin* is strong enough to survive and thrive, making people laugh and bringing them together around whatever passes for a gaming table in the strange new world to come. ✳

Randy Scheunemann grew up as much as he was going to in small-town Minnesota, and joined the Navy when he was 18. After serving six years on a submarine based in Hawaii, he moved to Baton Rouge, Louisiana, where he worked on a riverboat casino repairing slot machines. This career stop was brief, and Randy moved back to Minnesota for a short time before relocating to Austin, Texas, where he began working for Steve Jackson Games as a shipping clerk. Since then, he has helped to create and develop several games, including *Zombie Dice, Revolution!, Mars Attacks: The Dice Game*, and *Mars Attacks: Ten-Minute Takedown*. He spends much of his time traveling to conventions as a demo master and speaking with store owners about SJ Games releases.

TELL YOUR OWN STORY

Upon Death, after the party has looted your corpse, you may go through the Door discards and choose one Class and one Race to put into play. Then go through the Treasure discards and choose 2 Hands worth of Items, 1 Headgear, 1 Footgear, and 1 piece of Armor that you could legally equip and put them into play. You still draw a new starting hand on your next turn.

MUNCHKIN AS MONOMYTH

Jaym Gates

Y ou'll be famous, *he said.* You'll be fabulously wealthy, *he said.*
All the gorgeous princes will be asking you to the ball, *he said.*
What a load of bollocks.

*I mean, really. Look at this place. It's a midden, not a dungeon.
I'm pretty sure even rats have higher standards than this. But there's
me, wishing over the well one morning that I might have some sort of
adventure, and next thing I know, some old guy
with a posh accent and tatty robe is standing on the roof of my nice little house,
using his staff as a lightning rod and
proclaiming something about destiny.*

*So, here we are, a bunch of bewil-
dered strangers herded together by Sir
Arsed, each of us tasked to find the Great
Hoard of Immense Beauty, and not a one
of us has the slightest bloody bit of interest in entering the dungeon. Who does
this? Who looks at a filthy dungeon and
says, "Oooo, guvnah, let's have a stroll*

about and see if we can't find some nice, quiet dragon, bash it about the head, and be home in time for tea? We can use the gold plate, today, I think."

* * *

A few years ago, I had the chance to interview Jack Gladstone, a Native American elder from the Blackfoot tribe. I was writing about the tradition of oral storytelling in the modern age, and he agreed to speak with me about the subject by phone. He was driving through Montana at one point, and pulled off the road to stretch his legs, talking to me the whole time about how stories were the fabric of human experience. They were schools and churches and comfort on long, dark nights. But what I remember most is the *experience* of the interview. His voice wove a narrative that went beyond mere information, tapping into some emotional wellspring that is usually reserved for the best books or movies.

Sharing stories is, indeed, a primal experience. Even within a novel or short story, the author will often sit the characters around the fire for a ghost story, or have them tell stories while they travel. Think in particular of *The Canterbury Tales*, where the pilgrims spend most of the work telling one another stories. Done poorly, it's a cheap tactic to shovel backstory or a moral into the tale. Done right, it's a chance to give the reader an engaging experience that brings them into the characters' world even more intimately.

As readers or listeners, we are constantly being engaged in what Joseph Campbell called "the hero's journey," in its most basic form – or, in more academic language, the monomyth. Campbell summarizes the idea in *The Hero with a Thousand Faces*: a hero ventures forth from the common world into a region of supernatural wonder; fabulous forces are there encountered and a decisive victory is won; the hero returns from this mysterious adventure with the power to bestow boons on his or her fellow man. These concepts aren't limited to one time or culture; we are continually expanding, rewriting, evolving, and retelling the same basic stories that have always been told, putting our own cultural stamp on them before passing them on to the next generation to shape.

Even a short survey of many classic works – particularly in speculative fiction – shows a widespread adherence to Campbell's model. *Beowulf*, *The Odyssey*, and even the original Star Wars trilogy all follow the pattern. That's not to say Campbell's is the *only* pattern, though. There are many dissenting voices that criticize his work as applicable only to a certain Western subset of stories, barring women and non-Western themes from the discussion. Charlie Jane Anders, in a piece for io9 titled "New Proof That Every Sci-Fi Epic Is Based On Joseph Campbell," calls the monomyth "a cookie-cutter spiritual-ish adventure recipe," while Film Crit Hulk explains on her website that her main problem with *The Hero with a Thousand Faces* is that "our society has overtly adopted the book's breakdown of the hero journey as some kind of ready-made app for 'paint by numbers' storytelling."

The beauty of the monomyth concept, however, is that it is absolutely malleable, and, as with anything, its power lies in what you do with it – particularly in gaming.

* * *

You know, in hindsight, when you're thrust into a highly suspicious magical adventure, never allow yourself to be elected the scout.

I was just walking along, minding my own business, when WHAM! this screeching thing attaches itself to my head. And my weapon is a Big Rock. There are times when the solution hurts more than the problem. . . .

I don't even want to be here. I didn't know how hard it would be to step over that threshold into a dungeon that could hide anything from treasure to eldritch horrors. I used to love listening to the stories of Margian Godbane, Harran the Bold, and the great adventurer Encilia. As a

kid, as just another farm girl in a remote part of this most minor of minor kingdoms, I whiled away the days, dreaming of traveling to the halls of elven kings and the depths of dwarven strongholds, fantasizing about bards writing of my bravery, and wallowing in the imagined glory of returning to my village as a household name.

Instead, I have a dead Psycho Squirrel attached to my head, and all I got out of the conflict was a Rat on a Stick. Never trust a Bard. Or a Wizard. They're all in it together.

I wonder how my beloved Wizard would feel about a Large Angry Chicken in his bedroll tonight? I know I'd feel immensely better if that were to come to pass . . . even if he turns me into a frog.

* * *

To a creator of any sort, the monomyth offers a sort of loose recipe that brings together familiar ideas and processes for making a heroic tale that will speak to audiences and engage their emotions. But there's more to using it than just following a preset list. The challenge for the creator is to sort out the ingredients she wants to use, making her own final concoction for her audience to enjoy.

And this is where *Munchkin* comes in: if you draw a handful of cards, there's a story in them. All the pieces of the monomyth are there, too, but tossed into an unpredictable order in every game. It's the monomyth in tasty, funny, bite-sized pieces – even if your personal choices in telling this story seems no more complex than deciding whether to loot the room or open another door, or choosing between the Cheese Grater of Peace and the Chainsaw of Bloody Dismemberment, and your journey through hell lacks the strange tangents of gods and sirens (usually – *Munchkin* is nothing if not surprising with the monsters).

Odysseus would have loved a *Munchkin* hero's journey, come to think of it.

There's more to it than that. Your fellow players are also influencing your story, taking the parts of antagonists and allies. Your struggle is against the game *and* against them, putting you directly in the shoes of the hero in a way that few other games do, and damn that player who adds 30 extra points to the Large Angry Chicken you're about to kill to win the game.

Munchkin also shakes loose the focus on the character arc, and reminds the creator that the real power of a story is in its details. The basic plot exists to fulfill the character and offer impetus for her transformation, but it's the details of that transformation that connect the audience to the story in the most meaningful ways.

* * *

It's interesting how quickly you become blasé about monsters. We've been adventuring through this vile dungeon for days now, making camp in the safest rooms, kicking in doors, slaying monsters, triggering curses, looting corpses. It's almost . . . enjoyable, in a sick way.

The monsters are getting bigger, and my weapons have gotten better. I've got a Swiss Army Polearm now, and it's awesome. I can slice, bash, eviscerate, whip, open, screw, or clean the nails of just about any monster we find. My armor is incredible, too, if inexplicably jewel-encrusted.

And I even got a little dragon! He's so cute, although he keeps crisping my locks. My companions finally made me cut my hair short. Something about how awful burned hair smells.

I kicked down a door today, though, and found out why the Wizard wanted us with him.

I always did want to be cannon fodder, truly I did.

* * *

As the comics character Charles Xavier, leader of the X-Men, says, "In mutant heaven, there are no pearly gates, but instead, revolving doors." Death and resurrection are so common in pop culture franchises that they're almost a running joke. Done too often, death and rebirth becomes cheap and shallow, robbed of all its pathos, drama, and emotional punch – the very antithesis of the role death is intended to play in the monomyth. Comics are particularly egregious in their abuse of the resurrection plot device. Mutant Jean Grey is constantly dying and coming back when needed. Instead of moments of growth, change, or evolution, these events become static points on a map, her passage unmourned by readers because they know it is only temporary. Hey, even when a character is only "on screen" for a few moments, his death should mean something to someone.

The same sort of criticism can be aimed at so-called Shakespearean deaths, with their drawn-out monologues and endless reprises. A good death scene is subtle and spare, or a short, hard punch. We all understand the emotions surrounding death, and with the right balance of information, a storyteller can tap the audience's own experiences with death, in whatever form, to color in their scene, making it far more powerful than the most extended, violent, visceral demise.

Of course, sometimes a good death scene can be lightened with a little irony. You don't want the scene to be funny, but gallows humor can go a long way toward keeping a dark story from becoming all-consumingly grim.

And when it comes to funny, look no further than *Munchkin* for an illustration.

* * *

I don't even know what the thing was. Unspeakably Awful Indescribable Horror, maybe, and apparently it really likes the taste of Warrior. I didn't stand a chance. One moment it's there. Next thing I know, it has wandered off and I'm lying on the floor, bleeding out, while everyone loots my gear. Seriously, these are my "companions" on this adventure?

* * *

The presence of death and rebirth in *Munchkin* speaks to the idea of character death – real or metaphorical – as a new beginning, something found in tales ranging from the epics about early Celtic gods to Mesopotamia's Ishtar to King Arthur to Batman. In *Munchkin*, the deaths are funny, of course, but they're also an opportunity for a player to take the reborn character on a vastly different path, to rip her feet out from under her and send her spinning in a new direction. True death – again, whether metaphorical or physical – should strip the character of everything that came before. Upon rebirth, their priorities, hopes, connections, even their way of thinking may be different.

This can be done as a reboot to a character who has lost hope or motivation, or to one who has become complacent in wealth, comfort, or privilege. It is one of the reasons we so often see stories beginning with the death of loved ones – it isn't just the hero's death that creates this precipitous change – and it all too often becomes a shorthand for emotional turmoil.

While this can be handled well, it's a character-building device that must be used sparingly, and with care. Death is not the only way to push a character forward with haste and worry. Tolkien's Bilbo had the weight of the world resting on him when he ran out his door without a handkerchief, but he didn't know it yet, and a beautiful, powerful story was created without ever killing off the hero or his loved ones. Sometimes the threat of loss is greater than the actual loss, which is where the metaphorical death comes into play.

In *Munchkin*, you don't *really* die. You just lose all of your stuff. But you are set back, weaker, vulnerable to even lower-class baddies and to your fellow players. It's the same thing when a character suffers a world-changing event – amnesia, robbery, assault, the loss of home or loved ones – their defenses are gone, along with their carefully constructed habits of survival, and they are left shivering in the night while wolves howl around them.

Death, that king of chaos, is a great thing to inflict on characters or players who are becoming too complacent and safe with their piles of treasures and weapons, or their worldly knowledge. It shows that even the mightiest hero can be brought low. Physically, mentally, emotionally, death is transformative and wrenching, forcing the character to face her darkest self. When she comes back, she is remade, but that transformation can go many ways, from Batman's dark, vengeful force, to Doctor Who's erratic playfulness, to the pious, controlled peace of Zotoh Zhaan, of *Farscape* fame.

Whatever the result, the death and rebirth must be a pivotal moment for all involved – the hero, supporting characters, creator, and audience.

*   *   *

Wait, I'm alive? I know I was dead . . . I had this long talk with another old guy in a white robe, and he said something about me not being done with my journey. So, now I'm lying here, completely confused, and guess what? Still don't have my stuff.

The party refused to give up the weapons and armor and other goodies they looted from me when I fell, so my dragon and spear are gone, but I got a tinfoil hat and an axe. They will have to do. I have a WHATSIT to slay and a treasure to claim.

If I make it out of here alive, may the gods smite me if I ever enter another dungeon or listen to another Wizard.

Hmmm. I wonder if the treasure includes any Wizard repellant?

* * *

The hero's journey can last any length of time, from a few days to a lifetime. It can take many paths and many shapes, but in the end, the branching narratives line up to tell us one thing: it is human to quest, to look for a journey, to embark on that path and discover the best and worst of what we are, and what we can do. While life doesn't usually include ducks in dungeons, I've met more than a few murderous potted plants, and there's nothing funny about an overgrown asparagus fern next to the front door.

So next time you're playing, take a closer look at those cards. There's a whole lot of history behind them, a whole lot of storytelling magic, and it's spelled out in the language of Maul Rats and Staffs of Napalm. ✳

Jaym Gates is an author, editor, and communications specialist. She has a lifelong horror of potted plants thanks to traumatic early experiences with an asparagus fern and would like to ask that the monster be reclassified as level 20. More information on the non-potted plant parts of her life and career can be found on her website jaymgates .com or Twitter @JaymGates.

IGNORE THE RULES

You may equip all items you have carried when you use this rule, ignoring legality. Afterwards, you cannot add more unless it would be legal.

FROM CANDY LAND TO MUNCHKIN

THE EVOLUTION OF A YOUNG GAMER

Dave Banks

L ike most fathers, I was overjoyed when my kids were born. My happiness might have been more than others', not because I loved my kids more than other dads did, but because I had more of a reason to be thrilled. By twist of fate and embryonic cell division, I am father to triplets: identical girls and a boy.

It's been an interesting road and probably not all that different from the one that other families travel; we just go through things all at once and in a big way. Like braces and puberty and diapers. We went through a lot of diapers.

To be honest, the first couple of years were pretty boring. Sure, the many late-night feedings were an amusement park's worth of fun, and three tykes crawling (and then walking) in three different directions certainly kept us busy, but I couldn't wait for my kids to get old enough to really interact with us and, more importantly, play games with me.

I have the somewhat unfortunate situation of being a gamer married to a non-gamer. I'm not complaining. My wife will occasionally sit down for *Scrabble* or backgammon or one of "my games," like

Agricola or *7 Wonders*, but given the choice, she'd rather read or do something else. So I was excited that I had three potential additions to family game night in development.

As my kids grew older, I eased them into gaming with traditional fare. We played the staples – *Candy Land* and *Trouble* and the like – as many times as I could bear before getting bored and frustrated. I also peppered our sessions with nontraditional designs for younger players, such as *The Magic Labyrinth* and *Gulo Gulo*. Unfortunately, no matter what I tried, my daughters just weren't that interested. I could draw them in once in a while, but they seemed to take after their mother. That was okay. I'd rather have an occasional player than someone completely shut off to gaming.

The silver lining was that my son loved games. I mean he *really* loved them. As soon as I would get home from work, he'd want to play. This was fantastic; how could I ever say no? Granted, I'm sure some of it was him just wanting to hang out with Dad, but I was happy to be sharing my interest in gaming with him.

It was really interesting to watch how he *played* games early on. While we might use the rules as written, he would always want to continue interacting with the game afterward, but without the

rules. A session of *Candy Land* devolved into a battlefield with the blue and green tokens forming a coalition to fight red and yellow. Cards were propped up against each other to form bunkers and artillery guns. The same was true of other games. Without his ever having seen it played, he made *Monopoly* a racetrack and *Munchkin* another battle-field, its tokens far more warlike than the smiling children of *Candy Land*. While he was too young to play, the colorful pawns faced off in armies. Rolling the die to the Munchkin face meant certain death for the enemy.

Designs aimed at kids his age were important for him developmentally. He needed to learn how to win or lose gracefully and to be patient when it wasn't his turn. There were also cognitive skills, such as pattern recognition, that he needed to master. But the one thing that truly revealed itself during all these early experiences was imagination – creativity in finding ways to try to win and, during free play after the "real" game was done, in how he used the components. His experience was unique compared to his sisters', who would play a game as quickly as possible, only to move on and have similar experiences through drawing or interacting with other toys. In a sense, they were already roleplaying, but while my daughters reached for crayons or American Girl dolls, my son tested out new roles and acted out his feelings with game pieces. When the red Munchkin had finished his race to level 10, he was ready for an all-new battle, one that involved chainsaw sounds, screams, and bloody victory.

As my son grew, we tried new and different titles. Now, I admit that I was always pushing the boundaries of what he might be ready for, but even with that in mind, it was a frustrating search. I love the idea of the ubiquitous international symbols on the corner of almost all game boxes these days – the ones denoting how many players the design is best suited for, how long an average session will take, and the recommended ages. Unfortunately, with the exception of the number of players, I've found that the information is quite often wrong. I've played some games that take twice as much time as is listed on the box and others that are over in a fraction of the projected time. That's fine. Maybe we socialized more than usual for those marathons or missed a rule that significantly shortened the games that ended too soon. No real complaints there. But the your-mileage-may-vary quality of the labels meant it was a challenge to find titles that were appropriate.

My reasoning for some purchases was undoubtedly flawed because of an assumption that a game intended for ages 10 and up had to be okay for my intelligent and engaged seven-year-old. Seems logical, right? In many cases, it was true. He "played up" on some titles aimed at slightly older kids and did quite well. With others, the age recommendation held firm; I could see his mind wander, or I recognized that he was pretending to understand when I knew he didn't. Those failed experiments were relegated to the closet for future use. For a lot of games, though, the suggested age ranges proved unreliable. Some are rated for older kids based on content, while others have mechanics that are more difficult for kids to grasp. The only reliable method for determining appropriateness for my son was to just sit down and try the game out.

Which we did, as often as possible.

Sometimes we would play for half an afternoon, jumping from box to box, table to floor and back again. Other times, we would just concentrate on having fun and enjoying each other's company. I'll admit that there were quite a few weekend afternoons when we spent more time just having make-believe battles with *Heroscape* tiles and figures than ever actually playing the game.

In my quest for new possibilities, I scouted the aisles of my friendly local hobby store, looking for titles that we might be able to enjoy. More often than not, I could only see the limitations. I was left to dream of playing all-weekend wargames with him or, flipping through a stack of *Dungeons & Dragons* modules, to long for the day when we could experience RPGs together. I knew Wizards of the Coast recommends players get started with *D&D* around age 12. I was close to pulling the trigger and giving it a go, but I wasn't sure our boy was quite ready to sit at a table and focus on a single encounter for an hour or more.

Then inspiration struck and I realized that, perhaps, it was time to introduce him to a "real" game of *Munchkin*.

I talked my wife into being our third and she, my eight-year-old son, and I sat down to play. The rules were easy to teach him and, before long, we were building our characters and leveling up. We were killing the monsters and stealing the treasure, as the *Munchkin* box cover advertised, but we ran into some trouble with the whole "stabbing your buddy" part.

Trouble arose when my wife or I played cards against my son; he perceived it as a personal attack, not at all like the mock combats he'd staged with the *Munchkin* tokens or the *Candy Land* pawns. He didn't understand why his mom and dad would work against him, to try to prevent him from winning. What's more, if I assisted my wife in battle against a monster, this was another affront. We were obviously teaming up against him. It quickly became evident that it was time to take a break from *Munchkin* and try something else. We played a cooperative boardgame and waited for things to cool down.

After a while, I had a conversation with my son. He was upset because he thought we were hurting him on purpose. The mechanic of working against your competitors was new to him and the idea of his parents working against a kid while working together without him was simply too strange and confusing.

Sadly, *Munchkin* went back in the closet for a while.

Our first experience with *Munchkin* weighed heavily on me – while I knew it could be a lot of fun, my son didn't. I still wanted to get him back on the Undead Horse (kicks, bites, and smells awful, lose two levels), in a manner of speaking. So I started thinking about the *Munchkin* experience and similar games and mechanics.

Since *Munchkin* is a dungeon crawl, I thought perhaps there were lessons to be learned from a traditional RPG. One Saturday afternoon, we sat down at the kitchen table. I asked him what he liked about games and what he didn't like.

"I really like make-believing about fighting monsters," he began. So far, so good.

"And pretending to be a knight or a fighter on an adventure." Getting warmer.

"But I like it better when we're on the same team and don't hurt each other."

Full reverse!

He was most of the way to being not just a *Munchkin* fan, but a full-on adventure gamer. However, I didn't want to push him too far, too fast. I knew there was a solution, and I found it in my own childhood and a very special red box.

With a couple of his neighborhood friends, my son sat down with me to learn how to play *Dungeons & Dragons*. Over the course of quite a few weekends, we began a journey to discover just how much fun roleplaying games could be. In my son and the other boys, I saw my own 10-year-old self, paging through the *AD&D Player's Handbook* in the basement of a friend's house, slowly making sense of the arcane formulas and charts with rows of numbers. More importantly, I saw the excitement grow in each of them as they tentatively explored caves and dungeons. They challenged their imaginations as they considered all the possibilities that lay before them.

It was magical and it was gloriously fun. But I had another agenda. Besides just learning how to play an RPG, I also wanted to show my son how brutal these kinds of games could be. More than once during that adventure, his character, a cleric, was attacked mercilessly by kobolds, skeletons, and goblins. He came close to dying a couple of times, only to be rescued by his comrades – or, I have to admit, a suspiciously low dice roll by the DM.

In this cooperative environment, my son could explore the boundaries of RPGs, yet still feel somewhat protected by his allies. As the adventure continued, the kids reached out, trying to find the limits of what their characters could do. Not surprisingly, this included attacking each other – and, subsequently, discovering the repercussions of such an action. At first the self-destruction of the party was greeted with anger and disbelief.

"Can he do that?" asked one boy.

"Sure, why not?" I replied in my best mischievous-DM voice.

The table was silent as the kids worked out what had happened and how they might react.

"Can I hit him back?"

"Absolutely."

The stage was set for a return to *Munchkin*.

We still finished the red box adventure and had a wonderful time doing it. It led to a lot of things: a *D&D* campaign that lasted nearly a year, a love for painting miniatures, and an interesting request the following week.

I was reading a book when my son came into the room. "Hey, Dad," he started. "Do you think we could try playing that *Munchkin* game again?"

"Absolutely."

Now that he was battle-tested, I thought the next crack at *Munchkin* was sure to be different – and was it ever. When we sat down to play, my wife and I planned to take it easy on him. He would certainly take it easy on us. My son, however, had other plans. He came out swinging, not necessarily all that interested in leveling up, but mostly intent on putting a little revenge smackdown on Mom and Dad for the earlier session.

He benefited from a seemingly never-ending draw of lucky cards to bolster the monsters we were battling. Our combat strength failed time and time again, and he cackled away, very pleased with himself. I smiled, partly at his joy, partly at the knowledge that the gamer training wheels – and the gloves – were coming off. The session eventually ended, although it certainly ran much longer than a typical game, and *Munchkin* found its way into our regular rotation.

But not just the core set. Of course not. We had to pick up expansions and variations like *Munchkin Axe Cop* and *Munchkin Zombies*. For a while, it seemed like we couldn't visit our local game store without coming home with a foil pack of *Munchkin* cards.

At first my son wanted to build the most serious, damaging character. He wanted a Warrior with a sword, a helmet, and a shield. But eventually the Bad-Ass Bandana (+3 bonus, usable by human only) won him over and seriousness gave way to silliness. He spent game after game trying to build the wackiest but still most powerful character he could, complete with Boots of Running Really Fast (+2 to Run Away) as a means of last resort. Many an evening or weekend was spent constructing these absurd and goofy characters, then banding together to kill Plutonium Dragons and Unspeakably Awful Indescribable Horrors or just throwing a spanner in someone else's plans.

We'd mix and match the cards to create humongous door and treasure decks, and giggle at the unpredictable combinations that came about as a result of combining the many sequels and expansion packs. A Cleric with Decaying Flab, a Sunday Bonnet, and Stick to Human Boots? One of us probably played it at some point. Some of the most outrageous combinations have produced some of the finest results, and all the laughter coming from our *Munchkin* free-for-alls has actually made my daughters more interested in playing. They aren't head over heels like my son, but I'll take what I can get.

Unfortunately, more responsibilities for me have resulted in less and less play with my regular group. But I still find time for a weekly game with my son and one or two others. It's interesting to note that, while my playing time has diminished a bit, his hasn't. He's become a bit of a *Munchkin* evangelist, spreading the word and turning his friends on to the game by explaining the rules and breaking open the box at every opportunity. It's with a good deal of pride that I watch him gift *Munchkin* sets at nearly every birthday party he attends.

Some afternoons, my son will sit at the dining room table, sorting through the decks, trying to cobble together the most ridiculous or powerful character possible. It reminds me of our idle play with *Heroscape*, ignoring the rules and just getting lost in the components.

Ultimately, this is what gaming is about to me. Winning and losing doesn't really matter; even after the worst defeat, I know that I still got to spend time playing with my family or friends. And as I watch my son rearranging cards by himself, using his imagination and just having fun, I appreciate games even more. It's good to forget the rules for a while and just enjoy your own version. Eventually, though, the need for interaction – and competition – returns.

"Hey, girls," my son calls out to his sisters, "want to play *Munchkin*?"

"Sure!" they yell back.

Smiling, I walk toward the table. I know there's always room for one more. ✴

Dave Banks is married, has three kids and two dogs, and lives in Kansas City. By day, he is an advertising executive, promoting goods and services across the web and in trade magazines everywhere. By night, he writes for the *GeekDad* blog, covering everything from robotics to movies to games. Mr. Banks is also a nationally recognized speaker, talking about families and technology at conferences from coast to coast, including the Penny Arcade Expo and SXSW. His many interests include Formula One and Major League Soccer, but above all else, he is a born-again tabletop gamer, converting others to cardboard and living by the mantra, "Hey, even if you lost, you still got to play a game. And that's a pretty good thing." You can follow him on Twitter at @davebanks.

MUNCHKINIZER

Double the combat bonus of any physical *Munchkin* swag such as shirts, figures, or dice you are using during this game.

THE EMPEROR OF FUN

AN INTERVIEW WITH PHIL REED

Matt Forbeck

Phil Reed is known most widely these days as the chief executive officer of Steve Jackson Games, but he's also a highly regarded game designer, graphic designer, and publisher in his own right. He started in the hobby industry in 1995 and served his first stint with Steve Jackson as, among other things, a production artist, from 1999 to 2004. He subsequently spent plenty of time on projects for other companies, in a variety of roles, giving him the kind of perspective that a lifetime employee of a single company might find hard to cultivate. After running his own publishing venture – Ronin Arts – for a number of years, he returned to Steve Jackson Games in 2007.

In 2008, Phil became the company's chief operating officer, second only to Steve Jackson himself. He has helped helm the company ever since, guiding it through several of its most productive years, thanks in no small part to the success of *Munchkin* as a game and as a brand. In late 2014, Steve Jackson moved aside and made Phil the company's new CEO, in recognition of Phil's hard work and incredible business acumen.

Honestly, the word *coup* never came up.

Phil also moves so fast and handles so many things that he's damn hard to pin down long enough to answer a few friendly questions. I'm told a subpoena might work, but first I'd have to find something to file suit for. Sadly, my attorney doesn't think emotional distress from having my kids beat the pants off me in *Munchkin* constitutes solid grounds, even with some judicious judge shopping.

Despite having to give up that excellent Plan A – which would have included Phil answering questions *under oath*, I point out – I did manage to compile the following interview by contacting Phil via Twitter, Slack, Facebook, Instagram, Snapchat, WeChat, Medium, text message, Google Hangouts, crossword puzzles in *The New York Times*, and even an unfortunate experience with AOL Chat.

His responses have been cobbled together into what follows. Some of it might still make sense. The rest of it probably never did. If you're baffled, just assume the joke somehow went over your head and roll with it. That's what works for me.

In any case, here's what Phil had to say about *Munchkin* as a phenomenon. Just don't be surprised if he tries to deny some of it.

What makes Munchkin **Munchkin***? I mean, including games and T-shirts and dice and whatever, when someone sees something with the* Munchkin *brand on it, what do you think they should expect?*

I think they should expect it to be very silly. If they're not laughing right away, then we've probably made a mistake with it. And I like it when they're surprised. It's fun when we do something people don't expect and it still makes them laugh.

That's better yet. Munchkin *started out being available only through specialty game stores. Over the years, it's gone far broader than*

that, expanding its reach into all sorts of venues. Where else can we find it now?

Right now, *Munchkin* is available through several specialty bookstores, through Toys "R" Us, through mass stores like Target and Walmart, and is still available through specialty game and comics stores.

What's the one place you'd like to see Munch-kin for sale where it's not available – yet?

AAFES stores [Army and Air Force Exchange Stores]. Definitely the AAFES stores. Or maybe Walgreens.

No, I know. CVS. Yep. Definitely has to be 7-Eleven. Wait.

Did you say only one? Can we rephrase the question?

I think you already did. Let's try another: How many languages is Munchkin *available in?*

Sixteen or seventeen? I'd have to look it up to know that number exactly. We've signed a few new licensees over the past year, and I can't remember what that brings us to.

Either way, that's pretty amazing. Any truth to the rumor that Munchkin *has been licensed for translation into Klingon?*

Klingon? No, no truth to that rumor at all. (Now Huttese . . .)

There's another rumor going around (that I may have started, just for the purposes of this interview) that the backstabbing action in Munchkin *is based upon the Christmas parties at the SJG offices. Any truth to that?*

I hate sore losers. I mean, uh, that rumor is a lie. It's kinda like cake in that sense.

Ouch! Munchkin *has been a massive hit, and it seems to keep growing in popularity. What do you do to make that happen – and to keep it happening?*

The biggest thing we do is to listen to fan feedback and try to create the sort of things they're asking for. And we encourage them to keep spreading the game themselves by telling friends about it and even teaching it.

The other big push that's helped grow the game has been moving into a larger distribution network with mass-market stores like Target and Walmart over the last three or four years.

The metrics we watch include not just the sales of the core *Munchkin* game but the sales of all the *Munchkin* supplements, too. We can look back between 2010 and today and see that, not only are the core *Munchkin* game sales climbing, we're also seeing a rise in all the expansions.

That's great news.

Right, and the expansions aren't available in Target, Walmart, or most Barnes & Noble stores. So we know that many people are finding the basic *Munchkin* game through those gigantic stores and having enough fun that they're hunting down local game stores for the expansions.

That's even better. That means you're drawing players in from the mass market to the hobby market, which is fantastic. That's a great growth curve for everybody involved.

Yeah, building the market like that is something we try to do every chance we get. We've updated our packaging and advertising over the past two years to include links to the Store and Gamer Finder on our site. We encourage people to use that to find game stores in their area.

I notice you're even advertising in comic books these days. I saw one in a Batman book.

We've been advertising in all Dark Horse comics for three or four years now, and it's always exciting to see the new *Star Wars* or *Hellboy* comic pop up with our ads in it. Recently, we added some Archie Comics advertising, and we just started advertising in DC Comics, too. That's a long-term ad contract we signed with DC, so you'll see those for many months to come.

How does this book (in which this interview will appear) fit in with your plans for Munchkin's *world domination? Or this essay? (And how have I somehow gotten myself tangled in this web?)*

We have *Munchkin* toys, comics, shirts, a *Munchkin* messenger bag, dice, boardgames, and even zipper pulls. Once, many years ago, there was *Munchkin Water*. This book gets *Munchkin* into a completely new category *and* places another publisher, BenBella, in the position of promoting *Munchkin*. But, you know, not in a manipulative way at all. That's right out.

That's a lot of merchandise. What do you do to tie it back to the game?

Since the very first shirt we created for *Munchkin*, non-game items have had in-game benefits. We did that in order to play on that whole concept of power gaming and munchkin-ing things. That way, we could encourage fans from our end to go out and buy the T-shirts from partner companies like We Love Fine. (And, again, we really do see these folks as partners. No manipulation involved at all.)

There's a promotional benefit from just having the fans wear the shirts, of course, but then they get an in-game benefit that we concoct for them, too. We created some promotional bookmarks for Mighty Fine; for other studios that publish licensed *Munchkin* games; for Funko, who make *Munchkin* toys. All those give you benefits in the game, so players have another reason to go out and support our partners.

I always thought that was a phenomenal bit of wisdom to say, "Hey, look. This is a game about manipulating the rules to your best advantage

– while having fun – and we're going to do the same thing with the merchandise." But people laugh about it! They're aware of what's going on, and they enjoy it, and they buy the things anyhow. One of my sons bought a Munchkin *figure, and he brings it with him to every game.*

Ha-ha! Another recruit for the *Munchkin* army!

The other thing we try to do, if possible, is include a new *Munchkin* card with those out-of-game items. With BOOM! Studios, for example, the issues of the *Munchkin* comic book may come bagged with a comic. I mean, with a card! That's funny! "Yes, the card comes bagged with a comic book!"

For some fans, that's maybe the right way to put it. When I wrote the Magic: The Gathering *comics for IDW, I know that some* Magic *fans would buy the comics, pull out the cards, and then throw away the comics and walk away with the cards – because that's all they really wanted.*

Well, hopefully the *Munchkin* fans will read the comic, too, and not just throw it away.

I'm sure most of them will have fun with both of them. After all, that's the idea. There was a tiny but vocal minority of the Magic *fans who did toss the comics, I know.*

Yeah, the same thing happened in 1994 or '95 when Wizards of the Coast created a bunch of *Magic* cards for various gaming magazines. People would buy six or ten copies just to get the cards.

And that sure sold a lot of magazines! While it's a shame some people ignore the magazines, hopefully the bulk of them at least gave them a try. Switching to something less depressing than discarded (ouch!)

magazines, tell me about the Munchkin *Tavern promotion. I know you've run it at Gen Con, but has it shown up anywhere else?*

It's shown up a couple years now at Gen Con and one year at Origins, too. The idea was to move into an existing restaurant and brand it with *Munchkin*. We created menus that had special food items – which were existing items, but with really funny names – and artwork from John Kovalic. We also had placemats and coasters and signage with John's art on it. It really creates a hangout spot for *Munchkin* fans when they're at the convention.

I know my kids have enjoyed visiting it at Gen Con. A lot. Sometimes you need to get away from a big show like that for a little bit to take a break, but it's wonderful to know you can find a relaxing place based around one of your favorite games just a stone's throw away. That leads me to my next question. Can you tell me about the Munchkin *pop-up store? Steve Jackson Games opened one in New York this year, I believe.*

We had a pop-up store during the New York Toy Fair. That's a three-day event. Steve Jackson came in, John Kovalic came in, and *Munchkin* czar Andrew Hackard came in. We ran a *Munchkin* invitational tournament there. We had all kinds of *Munchkin* goodies for people to buy, and some free stuff we handed out.

The idea goes back again to "How do we make *Munchkin* bigger?" Well, in this instance, the pop-up store was on Restaurant Row in Manhattan, on 46th Street. The timing overlapped with New York Toy Fair, so while various buyers from different stores and chains were at the convention and going out to eat dinner, there was a chance they'd walk by and see this *Munchkin* store.

Which could give them all sorts of great ideas. That sounds like a wonderful bit of cross-marketing for you. Hopefully you got regular people wandering by who stopped to check out the store, too.

We were hoping we would get a lot of the *Munchkin* fans in the area to come on out and join us. Steve and John and Andrew don't really get to that part of the country together much. When I go to things like New York Comic Con, the fans always ask me, "When's Steve going to come out? When's John going to come out?" So, this was kind of like killing two munchkins with one stone. It all went very well.

What's the craziest idea for a Munchkin *project or item you've had to axe?*

Last year I would have said "*Munchkin* store," but I can now scratch that off the bucket list. I think second craziest (besides a *Munchkin* convention) would have to be a *Munchkin* animated Christmas special. I outlined the release idea, put some energy into tracking down costs, and even went so far as to describe the rough plot of the special. I think it turned out that we needed to increase *Munchkin* sales to something like twenty times the current monthly rate in order to make such a dream a reality.

The DVD/Blu-ray/4K/LaserDisc release, of course, would have included new *Munchkin* cards.

I still want to make this happen.

At least! I also noticed that Munchkin *is invading other games now, with* Munchkin *editions of fantastic games like* Castle Panic, Love Letter, *and* Gloom. *How does that work? How do you apply* Munchkin *to these different kinds of games?*

There's also *Munchkin Smash Up.*

Better yet.

In general, the idea is to take a fun game and then *Munchkin*-ize it by twisting things around. For instance, *Castle Panic* is, at its core, a very cooperative game with everyone working together to protect the castle from monsters. In *Munchkin Panic*, you're still working together to protect the castle, but there's going to be backstabbing involved because you want to make sure not only do you as a group win but that you personally do better than everybody else.

So we take these great games and *Munchkin*-ize them by bringing in some of those backstabbing and treasure-hunting and back-and-forth elements you see in regular *Munchkin* games. This really comes out of an earlier idea I wish we could have proceeded with: the *Munchkin*-izer. This was an idea for a package of accessories you could use with any game to add a little bit of *Munchkin* flavor to it.

That sounds like that would have been hilarious.
I hope we can still get to it one of these days because I think it'd be funny.

It would definitely improve Monopoly, *at the very least.*
Don't let Steve hear you say that. He's a huge fan of *Monopoly*!

I'm sorry to hear that. I have a long rant about how Monopoly *is one of the worst games that everyone's played. Steve and I will have to have that out at some point.*
I think that would make a great YouTube video to watch.

Ha! We'll have to set up a brawl in a ring or something at our next convention together. Let's get meta for a moment: How would you go about Munchkin-*izing* Munchkin?
I'm sorry. We make it a company policy not to discuss unannounced projects.

Of course not! Beyond that, though, I know you have the Munchkin Level Counter *for iOS and Android. We've seen excellent versions of* Magic: The Gathering *and* Settlers of Catan, *plus countless other translations of tabletop games into video games. Any plans to do electronic versions of* Munchkin?
That subject comes up a lot, but we keep running into two major problems. Time is the big one. There are so many different *Munchkin* things going on, and a video game would really require the kind of focus we just can't provide right now. The other one is that a lot of *Munchkin* is subject to player interpretation. A computer game isn't

going to allow that to happen. I mean, there are times when we're working on new *Munchkin* rules, and Steve and Andrew will tweak things just enough so that a rule is clear, but also so that you could read it in another way that allows you to argue about it with the other players so you can convince them that it actually means something else.

Right! That's part of the game's charm. It captures one of the original RPG tropes that Munchkin *is based upon. You can stop and say, "Wait a minute! Because this is in my self-interest, I think this rule should be interpreted this way." Of course, the other players are going to want to do it another way.*

Yeah! And a computer game isn't going to be able to allow that kind of give and take. They're not designed to be that variable.

So you must have lots of great ideas that you just haven't had time to implement for Munchkin.

So many! For one, we wanted to produce fortune cookies that each had a *Munchkin* rule in them.

That would have been fantastic! And hopefully delicious.

Mostly we just can't get to all the ideas because of time constraints. It's a lot easier to sit down and brainstorm up new promotional ideas than it is to actually sit down and create them all. It's more important that we keep the game in print and make sure that there are new expansions in the works than it is to chase down every fun idea we come up with.

Well, hopefully the team can find a bit more time now that you've become CEO. Speaking of which, what does this mean for Steve? What's he doing these days?

Currently, he's on a very long break. His first real break in over thirty years. After that, he'll decide what he wants to do. I'm hoping he decides he wants to leave more of the business stuff on my plate and take on more of the creative stuff himself, having fun and going to conventions and the like.

That sounds like it would fit everyone involved really well. If he wants to take a break of any length, he's certainly earned it, but having him charge back into the creative side would keep the fans happy, too.

Oh, he hasn't stepped back too much. We were talking about a new license over dinner the other day, and when I got up the next morning, I had a new game from Steve waiting for me in my email inbox.

Of course! And that's just how it should be. Hey, now that you're the CEO, does this mean you can create new cards and rules on the fly like Steve's been known to do? And will you use that power for evil or for good?

Shhhh. I have been doing this at conventions for years. And I only ever use my powers for one purpose: to entertain myself. ✳

Matt Forbeck is an award-winning and *New York Times* best-selling author and game designer with 30 novels and countless games published to date. His latest work includes the novel *Halo: New Blood*, the *Magic: The Gathering* comics, the 2014 edition of *The Marvel Encyclopedia*, the *Monster Academy* YA fantasy novels, and the upcoming *Shotguns & Sorcery* roleplaying game based on his novels. He lives in Beloit, Wisconsin, with his wife and five backstabbing children, including a set of conniving quadruplets. For more about him and his work, visit Forbeck.com.

LICENSE TO ILINX

Use this rule after any other player has lost a battle. You draw the number of Treasures indicated on the Monster card, select the one you want, and then discard the rest.

HOW PLAYING MUNCHKIN MADE ME A BETTER GAMER

Christian Lindke

"The great objection to infant gamers is not their age
as such; it's their influence on the market. So long as
companies can survive by churning out solo adventures
and talking down to customers, there will be no
incentive for them to produce material that really
emphasizes skilled role-playing, and the hobby's image
will remain ludicrous. Even WHITE DWARF is not
immune to the plagues of juvenilia. If the twelve-year-
olds can't play properly, why should we encourage them
to play at all? Leave them until they are 16 (at least)."

—Phil Masters, *White Dwarf* #73 (January 1986)

I've been a fan of *Munchkin* from day one. My library has a shelf
devoted to the ever-expanding series. If you could travel back in
time to interview an earlier version of "gamer Christian," however, he
wouldn't believe that he could ever come to love a game with that title.

I don't know precisely when the term *munchkin* was first used
to describe a style of play. It came into fashion in the late '70s and
early '80s as more young players entered the hobby. Unsurprisingly,
publishers jumped on the trend and began producing products such

as the *Dungeon!* boardgame and *Fighting Fantasy* gamebooks, which were expressly aimed at this new audience. Some older gamers were reluctant to accept younger players and the play style they seemed to favor, and started calling them munchkins.

It's true even today that many youngsters gravitate toward what Robin Laws and Glenn Blacow identify as "power gaming" – focusing on killing monsters, stealing loot, and getting more powerful by overtly manipulating a game's rules. Some don't like this play style because it tends to dominate other, more narrative-focused styles, and if the power player is young and inexperienced in some of the social niceties of gaming with others, conflict between players can become more likely. It's a legitimate concern, but press the most ardent critics of power gaming and you'll sometimes find folks who think there is a right and wrong way to play. And the munchkin style of play is, to them, definitely the wrong way.

For a time I was one of those munchkin haters. I believed that game sessions were to be taken seriously and that players should focus either on creating a deep narrative or making complex tactical decisions. I thought that power gamers were self-centered and incapable of working with others to create a positive shared experience. If someone wanted to be a True Gamer, they had to play "the right way."

I picked up this notion with my first RPG experience, which was run by a munchkin-hating gamer. I was 11. After years of playing

Candy Land and *Operation*, and building imaginary landscapes with LEGOs, I was eager to experience the joys of this new type of game – the RPG. The media-fueled mystique about *Dungeons & Dragons* had something to do with my enthusiasm. The moral panic about *D&D* was in full swing and I wanted an opportunity to play this mysterious game where you could *be* heroes like those I'd encountered in fiction and in film.

It's almost painful to think back to that first adventure. The GM was a friend of a friend, someone I didn't know all that well. But he supposedly understood how to run a *D&D* game and, more importantly, was willing to let a pair of preteens – me and my friend Sean – join in the fun. Once we got the okay, Sean created character sheets for us. He would play as Aragorn, the valiant ranger, and I would be Gandalf, the powerful wizard.

The adventure opened as many fantasy roleplaying adventures do: "You meet up at a tavern," the game master announced. The descriptions the GM used were good, but I was more than ready to fill in the details myself once the adventure got underway. I used my imagination to create a detailed medieval tavern. (To this day, I can still conjure up this imagined watering hole in my mind's eye.) As things moved along, I was a little surprised to find that the game master wasn't working from any notes; the plot he created was clearly ad-libbed. He made up rules on the spot, too. I had never played *D&D* before, but I knew the game had rulebooks. There wasn't a rulebook to be seen at our table. I was also pretty sure that *D&D* used dice, but our GM never rolled dice, not even when our characters were attacked by the monsters we encountered in the stereotypical deep, dark dungeon we'd set off to loot.

Within minutes we had slain a patrol of orcs and acquired their treasure. It was not a large trove, but the game master informed us that it contained a scroll. Gandalf was the only magic-user in the group, so I took it. I looked up at the game master and said, "I read the scroll to see what's on it." The game master looked at me with a wry grin and said, "You've been polymorphed into an axe beak. Hand me your character sheet."

We all took a break at that point. I didn't know what an axe beak was, so Sean and I went to his room to find a copy of the *Monster Manual*. When I saw the picture of the creature, I was heartbroken. I wanted to play as a powerful wizard, but now I was being forced to play as a goofy-looking animal. Gandalf was supposed to fight Balrogs, not stand around as some oversized, flightless bird. I heard the older gamers laughing at my predicament. That made me feel even worse.

I ended up staying in Sean's room. My personal "right" way of playing never allowed for the possibility of the absurd, and I felt mocked and dejected. Why bother going back to the game at all? Sean, being a good friend, stayed with me so we could play with some of his He-Man action figures. The more serious players continued the adventure without any interference from the kids.

I made the wrong choice. I did not embrace my inner munchkin.

If I had fully embraced it, I could have pulled a Robert E. Howard and made the character the most powerful axe beak in the world. Legends would have been told of Gandalf the Axe Beak, wielder of the Sword of Kas, destroyer of Magistherion's bane.

I call this "pulling a Robert E. Howard" after the pulp adventure master's contribution to "The Challenge from Beyond." Howard co-wrote the story with C. L. Moore, Frank Belknap Long, A. Merritt, and H. P. Lovecraft. Each author created a short section that ended in such a way as to leave the next author in a difficult spot. Howard had the challenge of following Lovecraft, who had turned the protagonist into a loathsome and gigantic pale-gray centipede. Instead of crafting a Lovecraftian scene where the protagonist weeps in madness, or walks away in defeat like I did at the *D&D* game, Howard turns the protagonist into the god-killing king of all the worm men.

He fully embraced his inner munchkin.

Sociologist Roger Caillois, in writing about play, lists four main classifications for the play experience. In his model, play can be

divided into competition (*agôn*), chance (*alea*), vertigo or dizzying euphoria (*ilinx*), and simulation (mimicry). While most who use Caillois' typology assume that games are primarily composed of competition and chance, *agôn* and *alea*, playing *Munchkin* taught me that many of my favorites incorporate elements of all four categories. The way in which those elements balance out in any individual game is controlled by the designer and also by the players.

To some, roleplaying games are primarily a competition, a contest between the game master and the players. The GM controls all of the bad guys and monsters, while the players control the heroes. A fair application of the rules determines the outcome. Chance enters the picture through the use of dice, but this sort of game play is more *agôn* than *alea*. It can be an enjoyable experience, to be sure, but game masters who view themselves as an antagonist to the players often fall into the competition trap. They seek to defeat the players to the detriment of every other aspect of the game, and they find it rather easy to succeed, since the GM's chance of victory is limited only by the whims of chance and the roll of the dice. This was a common mind-set among game masters in the early days of RPGs – so common that Gary Gygax called out hyper-competitive GMs as "unscrupulous" and "unenlightened" in his book *Role-Playing Mastery*.

Fortunately, this isn't the only way to play RPGs. I rejected the strictly *agôn* paradigm early in my roleplaying career. So did my friend Sean. After our first misadventure with *D&D*, we tried eliminating the living game master completely. We played published modules as if they were solo tactical wargames, with our player characters working their way through the preplanned scenarios. This took care of the unenlightened and adversarial GM, but failed to satisfy our need for storytelling. Our play with the Masters of the Universe toys was more rewarding in that regard. We didn't realize it at the time, but the action figures allowed us to fluidly move between player and game master, alternating roles. We told collaborative stories where we challenged the characters, but not always in a strictly competitive way.

For the next few years I immersed myself in a variety of play experiences. I participated in baseball and soccer, and I tried out a wide variety of roleplaying games: *Dungeons & Dragons*, *Tunnels & Trolls*, *Star Frontiers*, and *Top Secret*. At first glance, they're very different

kinds of experiences. Sports require rigorous physical activity, while roleplaying and other games are primarily mental activities. Stealing a base and scoring a goal are physical achievements. They also create moments of *ilinx*, or vertigo. Soccer is a relatively predictable contest of ordered action as passes are made between players, but it is in moments of disruption that goals are scored. The scoring player feels an almost dizzying euphoria, caused by the successful disturbance and reversal of play up to that point. If you're a dedicated player, few emotional experiences compare with that euphoria, but the underlying sensation of vertigo isn't unique to that sport.

Nor is that feeling exclusive to sports. The *ilinx* you experience when scoring a goal is similar to the feeling you get when you successfully defend a vastly outgunned territory in *Risk*. You have only a single unit and your opponent has dozens massed at the border. You've not only beaten the odds when you defeat them, through a successful manipulation of *alea* (chance); you've created a moment of chaos by wiping away the most predictable outcomes. In both cases, the player experiences a rush of adrenaline and a mental state akin to vertigo. In the tabletop gaming environment, many games provide opportunities for reversal and chaos that create this sense of *ilinx*.

I was playing *Munchkin* when I first recognized how often a game could create emotional *ilinx* on a regular basis, one that wasn't always dependent on *alea*. The game itself is chaos and certain combinations of cards only add to the emotional vertigo, but before that revelation, I had to complete my quest to discover the "right" way to play.

My friends and I were still focused on games that were primarily a combination of competition and chance, with the occasional thrill of *ilinx*, but very little use of what Caillois identifies as simulation, at least overtly. We were unaware that we were incorporating the concept of mimicry in our play, nor would we have thought we were had someone asked us. We weren't openly adapting the stories we had read or the shows that we watched. Even our collaborative He-Man games didn't mirror the cartoons. Their narratives could be reduced to the simple formula of "open the door, fight the monsters inside the room, and take their stuff." While both wargames and action figure play incorporate Caillois' concept of mimicry, each form of play only highlighted half of what mimicry could be. The tactical wargames mechanically simulated the action of the conflict, while the improvisational play incorporated the narrative aspects of mimicry.

It wasn't until I'd read and played the *Fighting Fantasy* gamebooks by Ian Livingstone and Steve Jackson (the UK Steve Jackson) that I began to see how gaming could incorporate mimicry in a meaningful way. In my earliest RPG experience I had borrowed Gandalf's name, but the modeling stopped there. The fluid integration of game rules into the storytelling in the *Fighting Fantasy* series demonstrated how familiar narrative tropes could be wedded with mechanics to create a more immersive gaming experience. My initial forays into narrative gaming were quickly expanded when I learned how to play *Champions*, *Marvel Super Heroes*, and *DC Heroes*. Each of these RPGs contains a section about how to turn roleplaying sessions into narrative experiences. Games were about stories.

I had mastered all four of Caillois' classifications.

I was now, at last, a Very Serious Gamer.

And I needed *Munchkin* to help me have fun again.

Somewhere around the time I was going through my superhero RPG phase, I became a fan of John Kovalic and his *Dork Tower* comic strip. (To this day, Kovalic is my second favorite cartoonist; my favorite is my wife, Jody, but that's another story.) It was due to my love of *Dork Tower* that I purchased my first copy of *Munchkin*.

While the tagline "Kill the Monsters • Steal the Treasure • Stab Your Buddy" didn't particularly appeal to me – I've never been a big fan of screw-your-friends games – there was something about the chainsaw-wielding kid on the cover that did. I saw in him the polar opposite of the mopey magic-user who quit when he was transformed into a monster.

Opening the box, I found more tonic for my gaming soul. As I flipped through the cards, I came across "Pollymorph Potion," which depicts a hapless dragon being changed into a parrot. The bemused, disappointed look on the poor bird's face perfectly represented my own reaction to Gandalf's fate in my first RPG experience. It was almost as if Steve Jackson or John Kovalic had been participants in that long-ago game – or, more likely, they had sat through games where *ilinx* had reared its vertiginous head and dashed their hopes, too. Their answer to those kinds of disappointments is the real lesson here. They rush forward to embrace the impossible and the absurd, to answer the overly serious with whimsy.

As a game, *Munchkin* itself is quite simple. It simulates the dungeon crawl adventure so common among neophyte gamers: kick down the door, slay the monster, steal its stuff, level up, repeat. As a Very Serious Gamer, I'd come to believe that this simple narrative was monotonous and empty, but *Munchkin* transforms it into a zany good time.

There's more than jokes at work here, though. *Munchkin* features simulation, chance, and competition, and adds humor to the equation to create euphoric laughter. While the

"open door, kill monster, take its stuff" routine forms the basis of play, the game quickly shifts gears as players get more powerful. What begins as an enterprise of several solo adventurers seeking to make a quick profit transforms into a heated scrum where players ruthlessly undercut one another. Because *Munchkin* ends

if a player reaches level 10, as soon as one player
attains level 7 or so, they are now actively and
directly battling against the other players.
Here, the play is about preventing others from
winning. It is during this highly competitive and fast-paced endgame that some
of the most humorous and absurd card
combinations come in to play. How much
can you really complain when you're pre-
vented from winning, at least temporarily,
because you've been wiped out by an Intel-
ligent and Enraged Maul Rat armed with an Electric Radioactive Acid
Potion? In my case, not much.

It's hard to imagine a session of *Munchkin* that doesn't result in a
wild story you can tell the next time you're trying to recruit new players. The interaction of the cards creates narrative absurdities that beg
to be shared. And the possibilities are multiplied when you combine
cards from the various sets and expansions. Best of all, the glorious
madness of those tales stands as a reminder to even the most serious
Very Serious Gamer: be open to disruption and surprise.

Around the time that *Munchkin* was released, the third edition of
Dungeons & Dragons also saw publication. When I came to *D&D* this
time, I did so with the lessons that I had learned from *Munchkin*. It was
remarkable. I was finally able to create the gaming experience I had
hoped to have as a youth. The post-*Munchkin* me was looking beyond
the *agôn*, *alea*, and mimicry of my older play styles and attempting to
find a way to add *ilinx* to every gaming experience.

Munchkin is a great game in its own right, but it is a game that can
change the way that you play other games. In *Robin's Laws of Good
Game Mastering*, Laws notes that one of the best ways to play a game is
to make the experience as entertaining as possible for all participants.

Munchkin made me a better gamer, and if you're open enough
to the wild and wonderful experience, it can make you one, too. ✳

Christian Lindke is a renaissance geek whose motto is, "I can geek out about anything . . . except for Filk-singing." When he isn't working his day job as a nonprofit program director, or working on his PhD in political science, he can be found participating in one of his many hobby-related activities. He might be writing a new article for the *Robot's Voice* website or hosting an interview on his *Geekerati* podcast, which features interviews with screenwriters, game designers, and medieval historians. You might also find Christian working on his *Advanced Dungeons and Parenting* blog, though over time that seems to have much less to do with parenting than he intended. More often than any of that, Christian is probably playing games with either his regular gaming group or with his wife, Jody Lindke, and their twin daughters.

FLIRTING WITH DISASTER

For the remainder of this game, you gain the ability to force a player to help you in combat. After the monsters are killed, but before you draw treasure, roll a die. On a 1 or 2 your helper gets the levels and the Treasures, on a 3 or 4 you get the levels but your helper gets the Treasures, and on a 5 or 6 you get the levels and the Treasures. This may not be used for the winning level.

FLIRTING 101

THROWING THE DICE IN MUNCHKIN AND IN LOVE

Bonnie Burton

In a world of online dating and relating, it can be scary to interact face-to-face, away from avatars and screen names. Romance is tricky for geeks who have a hard time finding ways to meet others who share our love for dragons, swords, zombies, robots, and spaceships. Sure, we can attempt to make contact across a crowded room of cosplayers at a convention, but it's not easy to forge a love connection behind superhero masks and stormtrooper helmets.

How can a geek find a mate while displaying intellect, humor, and bravado? That's where *Munchkin* comes in! The best way to demonstrate your talent for wordplay, logical reasoning skills, and witty comebacks is to play a game. To succeed in gaming, you have to be quick in your reasoning as well as creative and imaginative. Flirting can seem like a paralyzing endeavor for some of us, but it's easier than you think to start up a conversation if you treat first-time interaction like a game in itself. Tabletop games encourage you to interact with both friends and strangers in a way that's much more rewarding than the usual bar scene or party.

Never jumped into a massive roleplaying game? You can skip all the background work they usually require and just play *Munchkin*. It's easy to learn, so you can spend less time stressing over rules and more time concentrating on how to win both the game and the attention of that intriguing person across the table. And for those of you lucky enough to have found a partner already, playing *Munchkin* can be a great way to rekindle the flirty side of the relationship, which humdrum day-to-day activities may have buried. Partners who play games together seem to have more fun.

Here are some handy tips on how playing *Munchkin* can be your gateway to making flirting fun:

1. CHOOSE YOUR MUNCHKIN GAME BASED ON YOUR FAVORITE OBSESSION!

There's a *Munchkin* card game for everyone. Love spy movies? There's *Munchkin Impossible*! Think vampires are sexy? Try *Munchkin Bites*! Love to fight crime? *Super Munchkin* is right up your alley! Hungry for brains? *Munchkin Zombies* is calling your name! Wanna show off your best robot voice? *Star Munchkin* is for you! The key is to pick a theme you already know a lot about so you can come up with the most knowledgeable and entertaining chitchat. If you're comfortable with the subject matter, you'll already be at ease for small talk. It's so much more fun to chat about zombies and brain matter with someone else who appreciates undead factoids and doesn't consider people who offer them creepy.

2. DUCK OF DOOM OR GLOOM?

Most people are either optimists or pessimists. In the *Munchkin* world, that places you in either the Duck of Doom or Duck of Gloom camp. Bring up the ducks in conversation to see which one your crush identifies with the most. You might discover they believe everyone should know better than to pick up a duck in a dungeon – it could be a devious, feathered-covered trap! Or perhaps they think the opposite is true, and you find out all ducks deserve to be taken somewhere more pleasant. Either way, it's a great conversation starter – and conversation is the best way to get to know someone better.

3. SIZING UP YOUR COMPETITION!

If you have discerning taste, chances are you'll have some competition not only in winning the game, but in winning the attention of your crush. The key here is to avoid looking like an ass when playing both the game of *Munchkin* and of love. When making jokes and challenging your opponents in witty banter, be careful not to go overboard. There's kidding and then there's not-so-charming kidding. Sexist, racist, or homophobic comments will definitely get you plenty of attention, but not the kind you want. No one likes to play with someone who crosses the line from entertaining to insulting. Being a jerk during a game sets you apart from the competition in the worst way possible. Back-and-forth banter is best when the remarks are more pithy than nasty. Think Humphrey Bogart in his film noir detective mode, Joss Whedon's heroes, or even Bugs Bunny.

4. Tell Funny Stories Based on the Cards You Draw!

This is your time to show off your bard skills. Got the "Shrieking Geek" card? Bring up that one time when you encountered a loud, screaming fan that pushed you out of the way to ask Mark Hamill for an autograph at a comic book convention. Ask others at the table if they have any crazy nerd tales to share, too. Or maybe you have to fight the Large Angry Chicken? Now's your chance to admit to the group that you kept your chicken Halloween costume just so you can occasionally wear it to amuse busy commuters by crossing busy streets. Use the cards to transition to life stories that spark conversation. When others realize there's much more to you than tabletop gaming skills, they'll be more apt to let their guard down and chat with you. A gaming table is most welcoming when it is treated as a shared storytelling space.

5. Listen and Learn!

You don't need to spend the entire session impressing players with your storytelling prowess, wit, and gaming acumen. Remember to listen so you can learn more about your table companions. Does the gal on your left get excited about certain monster cards? What kind of stories does the guy on your right tell when he gets "The Four Horsies of the Apocalypse" or the "Creature From the Pink Lagoon"? You can tell a lot about people from the monsters they prefer. When others have a chance to tell funny stories, unusual anecdotes, and *bons mots*, they let their personalities shine. Discovering people's passions, quirks, and eccentricities through their storytelling is half the fun when gaming with others.

6. HELP!

In *Munchkin*, you can ask another player for assistance during battle. This not only helps in game play, but also gives you an opportunity to interact with another player. Ask for help from that cutie you've been eyeing. But don't take it too personally if you only get a couple of gaming pointers and not much else. For some people, winning is everything.

Or better yet, offer to help another player out of a bind. Being a good sport goes a long way in *Munchkin* and in life. When you show that you're at the gaming table not necessarily to win but to have fun with new people, it will make others feel at ease around you.

7. BE AN ELDER GEEK GUIDE!

Does the person you like have a hard time understanding the game? Offer to sit out a few rounds and be a *Munchkin* sensei. Play "open" for a while, meaning with the cards face up. That way you and the others at the table can offer suggestions. Most new players will welcome the chance to play this way for a while, since it eliminates the pressure of having to learn the mechanics quickly.

There may be other opportunities to be of assistance, too. If the game theme is Cthulhu and the player is unfamiliar with H. P. Lovecraft, you can impress your crush with your knowledge of tentacles and Elder Gods. Even if the game is just a normal non-themed *Munchkin* deck, you can still help your crush figure out the best cards to play and what strategy to use to gain the most levels. When you offer to be someone's Jedi Master at *Munchkin*, your advice might receive appreciative attention. It can also be incredibly flattering to have someone spend so much one-on-one time with a newbie.

8. TIME FOR IMPRESSIONS!

If you don't act like a fool at some point when you're in love, you may not be doing it right. Someone who talks like a pirate occasionally during a session of *Munchkin Booty* is endearing. If you've got improv skills, now's the time to use them. But if you plan on staring hungrily at your crush during *Munchkin Zombies*, you may set the wrong impression. Watch the body language of the other players to see if you're being entertaining or just plain creepy. Every comedian beginning a daunting career in stand-up is told to know their audience. Watch other players carefully for their reactions to your behavior. If there's more laughing than eye rolling, you're golden. If your gaming crew prefers more subtle witticisms, keep the goofball antics to a minimum.

9. COSPLAY CAN BE CUTE!

If you really want to go full throttle in this flirting challenge, why not dress up in a costume worthy of the game you're playing? Wear a cowboy hat or a sombrero for *The Good, the Bad, and the Munchkin*! Dress in a tuxedo or a fancy evening dress for *Munchkin Impossible*. Superhero capes look impressive during *Super Munchkin*. And if you've got a Viking hat, by all means don it for the original *Munchkin* game! Wearing a funny chapeau or a costume shows that you're willing to embrace your silly side. Life can be too serious, so you might as well use a game of *Munchkin* to prove that you can throw caution to the wind.

10. THROW THE DICE!

Nothing reveals more about someone's personality than the type of dice they collect. All gamers have their special lucky dice, and

in the *Munchkin* world, there's a lot to choose from. Whether you prefer Jolly Jumbo, Rainbow, Radioactive, or Fairy Dust Dice, there's a selection that's just right for everyone. If you're hosting the game, you might want to have a bunch of different dice on hand for your fellow players. This shows you're welcoming and might even get you a sneak peek at your crush's inner desires, depending upon what gets picked. Dice always make for a fun gift. You can never have too many of them, and gifts of dice are a nice way to tell the special people in your life that you appreciate their gaming spirit.

11. DON'T CHEAT!

Remember all those old Western movies where they shoot the guy who tries to cheat during a poker game? Yeah, don't be that guy! Respect the people at the table with you. This should go without saying for any game. No one likes a cheater. (Unless you have the special *Munchkin* "Cheat!" card to play – that makes it okay!) When you cheat, your crush might wonder if you not only have problems with the rules of the game, but also the rules of life. No one wants to date someone who might cheat and break a heart.

12. BE ENCOURAGING!

If your crush plays a good hand, offer some praise. Thumbs up, high five, and sexy winking all work for successful flirting. A handful of confetti or glitter thrown in your crush's face might be going a bit far.

Try to keep your congratulations simple and sweet. This is especially important for those of us who are playing for the first time with a bunch of experts. (Nothing is scarier than learning a new game with a group of people who know all the tricks.) If you want to be the kind of person everyone wants at the table, offer some sincere kudos when another player figures out a complicated maneuver or bluffs like a gaming veteran.

13. ABOVE ALL, HAVE FUN!

When you let loose and are yourself in *Munchkin* – or any game – you show that you're comfortable in your own skin. Self-confidence and a good sense of humor go a long way in relationships. *Munchkin* is about fighting monsters, looting the treasure, and having a blast while being a goofball. There's nothing sexier than people who can laugh at themselves and help others have a good time . . . all while wearing Viking hats!

TOP 5 *MUNCHKIN* CARDS FOR FLIRTING

Need a great flirting springboard? Try playing these *Munchkin* cards for a chance to break the ice or at least have a reason to look good in front of your crush at the gaming table!

1. Friendship Potion
You play this card during any combat to discard all monsters. You won't gain any treasure and you can only use the card once,

but friendship is a great idea to demonstrate when you want to show your crush your softer side.

2. Yuppie Water

Is your crush an elf? If they ask for help, play the "Yuppie Water" card to help fight a monster, and you could end up being the hero of the battle.

3. Leather Armor

C'mon, everyone looks better in leather. Plus this is a

FRIENDSHIP POTION

Use during any combat. Discard all monsters in the combat. No treasure is gained, but the player may Loot The Room. Usable once only.

200 Gold Pieces

great way to bring up sexy armor as a conversation point. When else are you ever going to get to talk about it with your crush without looking too obvious?

4. Tuba of Charm

This card captivates your foes with beautiful tuba music so you can run away. In fact, if you successfully escape combat through your musical talent, you even get to grab a treasure card. When playing the "Tuba of Charm" card, be sure to mention what musical instruments you play in real life, or the ones you want to learn. Who knows, your crush could be an expert guitarist or pianist who'd be willing to teach you how to make sweet music.

5. Kneepads of Allure

Play this card to ask for help against a monster from someone special whose level is higher than yours – they can't refuse your request. While you can't gain the winning level in a combat if you use this card, it's still a great way to break the ice with someone you've had your eye on during the game.

Not Usable by Cleric
KNEEPADS OF ALLURE

No player with a Level higher than yours can refuse your request for help against a monster, or even ask for a reward. You cannot gain the winning level in a combat where your helper was compelled by the Kneepads.

600 Gold Pieces

San Francisco-based author **Bonnie Burton** writes about everything from Wookiees to mean girls. Her books include *The Star Wars Craft Book* (Random House), *Star Wars: The Clone Wars: Planets in Peril* (DK Readers), *Draw Star Wars: The Clone Wars* (Klutz Books), *You Can Draw: Star Wars* (DK Children), *Girls Against Girls: Why We Are Mean to Each Other and How We Can Change* (Zest Books), and *Never Threaten to Eat Your Co-workers: Best of Blogs* (Apress). Bonnie also contributed to *Womanthology: Heroic* (IDW Publishing), *Womanthology: Space* (IDW Publishing), and *The Girls' Guide to Guys' Stuff* (Friends of Lulu). Bonnie writes for CNET.com and *SFX Magazine*, and has written for *Wired, Star Wars Insider, Geek, Bust, Craft*, CNN .com, and *Huffington Post*. She hosts the web shows *Geek DIY* for Stan Lee's World of Heroes, *Vaginal Fantasy Book Club Show* on Geek & Sundry, and her vlog *Ask Bonnie*. Learn more about Bonnie on her site, Grrl.com.

CHARITY

Starting with the player using this rule, each player may give cards to the player on their left, until each player has had a chance to do so. For every two cards so given, the gifting player goes up a level. This cannot be used for the winning level.

THE CHARITY RULE

Colm Lundberg

I rish people, social bunch that we are, love poking fun at ourselves and each other. You know you've been accepted by the Irish community when we start to playfully insult you. No offense is intended; it's the way we communicate, the ubiquitous Irish *craic*. *Munchkin*, being a silly game (in the best sense of the word), plays right into that. The charming art, the self-deprecating card text, the daft things that happen during play – like when a hero fails and ends up wandering around holding a duck – all appeal to that style of interaction. Hindering a fellow player in combat through the timely use of a "Pretty Balloons" card or other forms of outright backstabbing fits well, too, as long as it is done in good humor.

There is more to *Munchkin*'s local success than just fitting into the Irish mind-set, though. *Munchkin* is one of those games that allows people to bond in a fun way, without recrimination for treachery. Its humor creates a space for people to share in-game jokes: all that communal laughter generates instant friendships!

Munchkin has so pervaded the Irish gaming community that it's not unusual at all to hear con-goers singing "Chicken on Your Head" to the tune of Rage Against the Machine's "Bullet in Your Head" or "Snails on Speed" to the tune of Duran Duran's "Girls on Film." To be certain, there are people who take their *Munchkin* seriously, but most Irish gamers prefer to have fun with the Potted Plant rather than debate over who should kick it out the door first. I can honestly say that

I have never been to an Irish convention where at least two sessions of *Munchkin* have not been going on at the same time, in different areas of the con, from side tables to demo tables and even in the pub.

I do not wish to add credence to the tired image of the "drinking Irish," but the social elements of our conventions are vital to their success. We gather as one community, one family, and enjoy ourselves dancing, drinking, gaming, and chatting as one manifold organism. And it is not a closed organism. One true representation of the Irish that we hear echoed from overseas is our welcoming nature, and at our gaming cons we have adopted many people from England, Scotland, the U.S., and even as far away as Israel. We come together in everything from pub quizzes to our famous charity auctions.

In fact, for many gamers these charity auctions provide the key social event of the convention. They've even gained an international reputation, reflected most clearly in their recognition in 2006 with the prestigious Diana Jones Award. This is an annual juried prize for "excellence in gaming," chosen by a mostly secret committee of industry notables. *Munchkin* is a crucial part of the auctions, but before I can show you how, you should understand more about how we run our conventions and our auctions.

Let's begin with our approach to guests of the convention. Rather than provide a rigid timetable of panels and a fixed schedule of events, we simply provide the guest a table, if they want one, and ask them to enjoy themselves. We feed and water them and make sure all the beer they get at the evening events is free. This initially leaves many guests astounded, since it's not the way most conventions work, but this approach allows them to become part of the community, play games they enjoy, and generally have (we hope) a fun, relaxing time. Our guests seem to like it.

Steve Jackson has been over here a few times. He was here at one notable Gaelcon in Dublin in October 1993 where the entire committee was leveled by a horrible flu. Only one or two committee members were able to attend each day and they were barely functional. Fans of the game *Illuminati: New World Order* will know of the quite rare "Irish Flu" card that came about from Steve's experience that year. There are other stories from 1993 about Steve and nightclubs that are probably best left to another time. . . .

Flu outbreaks aside, our convention guests often want to return, and when they do, they bring amazing lots to add to the charity auctions. Both Steve and *Munchkin* artist John Kovalic have seen the charity auctions in action firsthand. The mood of the event was so, dare I say, infectious, they even jumped onto the stage to join in as compères – or masters of ceremonies. Because I've had the honor of hosting the auction at the Gaelcon games convention for many years, serving as compère, I had the pleasure of sharing the stage with these crazy guys.

Running an auction of this kind is a uniquely humbling experience, and it's impossible not to be moved by the generosity the gaming community demonstrates through these events. We gamers spend our hobby time playing heroes. From our first choose-your-path game books to more in-depth roleplaying creations, we often want to play a character who makes a difference. The people who make these auctions possible give freely of their valued collectibles and offer bids to the maximum of their bankrolls. They *are* heroes. Most of them are quite humble, but raising over €30,000 at a single charity auction in the salad days, and even reaching over €15,000 in these recessionary times, is a pretty impressive achievement in anyone's book.

Let me give an example of the type of bidding that goes on:

- €1,200 for the right to be represented on artwork for a *Munchkin* card;
- over €1,000 for a copy of the old fanzine *Owl & Weasel*;
- €1,000 for 100 different comics, all less than a year old;
- €150 for some toilet paper I bought in a discount shop for €2;
- €50 to slap me;
- €800 for two bottles of whisky, one of which the bidder then put back into the auction to resell.

We tend to use the money raised to support children's charities, and much of the money goes toward buying games and toys. After the auctions conclude, the committees take photos and gather stories of where the money was spent, and bring both to the following year's event. One year, I was humbled to be there to provide a check to an Irish charity that provides therapy and support to young victims of sexual abuse. Posters made by the children lined the walls of the office. One was done by a girl aged eight. I still remember it, and the emotions it evoked, vividly. It was a simple poster, one color (bluish-green), with a single, powerful sentence in red paint: *I realize now it's not my fault.* I brought this picture to the following charity auction and put it on the projector behind me as I detailed its origins. People in the crowd began offering money before the first auction lot was even called.

The most *Munchkin*-focused charity auction in Ireland has to be at Warpcon in Cork, which runs every January. This is largely due to the regular presence of John Kovalic. John has attended so often that we see him less as a guest than as an errant friend who returns home for the show. John is a true gentleman, as anyone who has met him will attest, and the most obliging of people. He will sign and draw anything, on anything, for anyone (within the confines of legality and decency, of course). There was one year he could not attend, but he "deputized" me to be there in his place. It was the one year *Munchkin* products in Ireland went up in collectible value, since they were *not* signed by John.

John always comes prepared for the charity auction at Warpcon, often with original *Munchkin* artwork. (I am looking at the 10th-anniversary artwork currently hanging on the wall of my study as I write this.) Charity lots of original artwork are usually snapped up for bids never less than €700. He has also brought *Munchkin* boxes, card-holding suitcases from Germany, and many other collectibles from the world of *Munchkin*, including cookies, water bottles, bobbleheads, helmets, miniatures, and cuddly toys to beat the band. Through the items he has brought, John has singlehandedly raised thousands at the Warpcon auction.

There is one event – and I think it is right to call it an event – that John stages almost every year that tops the billing at the show and has every gamer slavering at the opportunities it presents: the chance to be part of one of John's published drawings. He has auctioned off the chance for people to be rendered as victims for My Little Cthulhu, a warm 'n' fuzzy Bringer of the End of the World, now also represented as a bonus card for the *Munchkin Cthulhu* set. The biggest draw, though, is the chance to be represented in a *Munchkin* card. That's right. In some of the sets of *Munchkin* you have on your shelf, one of the monsters or treasures or trap cards contains the image of an Irish gamer.

This all started about a decade ago, if memory serves, just after *Super Munchkin* came out and before *Munchkin 4: The Need for Steed* was announced. After witnessing previous auctions, John presented the idea to Steve, who readily agreed. To give you a small sample of some of the cards Irish gamers have become:

"Charisma" in *Super Munchkin*; "Bush Knife" and "Karate Training" from *Munchkin Impossible*; one of the "Super Munchkin" cards in *Munchkin Booty* (the pirate with a goatee and glasses, wearing red); as well as two cards won at the 2013 auction for *Munchkin Pathfinder*.

The "Bush Knife" winner is an archaeologist, frequently in the field, and the "Karate Training" card artwork depicts an actual martial artist!

The battle to be part of a piece of published *Munchkin* art unfolds like this. The auction has been going on for a few hours. Some beer has been consumed, and the bidding can be likened to the interaction of a *Munchkin* game. People in the audience – and the folks on the stage – hurl random abuse to coax bids higher or force rivals to back down, all in good humor, of course. By this point, the compère has little idea what lot is next or who has bid for what. (His or her job is to keep the show moving, and other volunteers thankfully keep track of all that.) Sometimes items are suddenly added to a lot to make it more appealing. Bidders who are rivals one moment may find themselves pooling their funds as a team the next, in order to win a treasure that has risen in value above their individual purchasing power.

The atmosphere in the room swings between jovial and electric – the excitement of the bids building, the joy when a lot is won, the cascade of good feeling and camaraderie in the crowd. There are no losers in this scenario and everybody knows that.

The people whose bids don't come out on top always congratulate the winners and they act as what we are: a genuinely close community trying to raise money for charity.

Into this scene strides the giant that is John Kovalic. (For those of you who haven't seen

John in person, he is well over six feet tall.) He takes the microphone and an image of Spyke, the iconic Munchkin, flashes up behind him. John starts speaking, and as soon as he mentions the chance to be immortalized on a card, hands shoot into the air with four or five fingers raised – an opening bid of that many hundred euros. John calls the bids; the auctioneer tries to keep track of the sea of flailing hands. Quickly the bid moves toward the €1,000 mark. Things get a little more serious now and people start talking. Artistic representation on a second card is entered into the lot. Bidders look for help, joining forces to secure the prized lot. A few moments later, the final bid is called. The treasure has been won, and the bar erupts in a massive cheer. A stunned John Kovalic shakes his head in humbled bewilderment as a pint is pushed into his hand. John and *Munchkin* have done it again. Winners of bids are grinning broadly, standing proud as the staff takes their details so John can arrange appointments for poses.

The chance to be featured on a *Munchkin* card has never earned a final bid below €1,000. Sometimes there are two cards, allowing a pair of gamers to combine resources and still take one card each. These lots have often gone for €1,500 or more. So we have the killer combination of the social community of gamers, a good cause for charity, *Munchkin*, John Kovalic presenting the lots in person, and a healthy sprinkling of Murphy's or Beamish. (Never drink Guinness in Cork; the aforementioned stout breweries are local.) The bidders'

wallets never really stand a chance – and they couldn't be happier about it.

Hobby gamers tend to personalize the games they enjoy, whether through house rules or by creating their own special storage cases for beloved titles and their expansions, but the Irish charity auctions afford devoted *Munchkin* fans a way to personalize their favorite game in special ways. Steve, John, and everyone at the company have been remarkably gracious in their support. It always makes me smile to think that there is a small part of the Irish game convention scene enshrined as part of the world of *Munchkin*. And because that facet is linked so intimately to charity and doing good for children, that connection is a +1 for us all. ✳

Colm Lundberg is a budding Irish writer who has been prominent in the Irish gaming scene for over 20 years. He's spent a lot of that time running charity auctions. He has also run charity auctions in the U.K., sharing a stage with James Wallis, who made a £50 charity donation to make Colm chug £3 fizzy wine. He has yet to forgive James. He managed to escape the capital city for more rural climes, currently living in the wilds of County Kerry with his wife Jen. They have a rescue dog called Scooby. (He is nothing if not original.) Colm has worked for Steve Jackson Games, has been a member of the MIB (Men in Black, the Steve Jackson Games convention support team) for over 15 years, and has learned many secrets during a stint as MIB Control. It is purely coincidental that he also works for the Irish government. Colm recently became a real-life game designer with his first game, *Love 2 Hate* from Green Ronin, and, no, he still doesn't know how.

BECAUSE I'M THE EXECUTIVE PRODUCER

Use during any combat, including your own. The combat is over. You get all the cards played during the fight other than the Monsters themselves. No one else gets anything.

MUNCHKIN HOLLYWOOD

Liam McIntyre

T V. It's a bright, shiny box filled with pretty pictures and good times. It's introduced you to a host of colorful characters and conflicts that have helped you escape the pressures of the real world. And sometimes, if the moons align, it brings people together.

Come to think of it, TV is a lot like *Munchkin*, which also comes in a bright, shiny box filled with pretty pictures and good times. It's a great way to escape the stresses of daily life and can bring people together. Why, I could even stretch this to encompass the whole entertainment industry, if I look at it just right. . . .

I think I'm on to something here.

Munchkin Hollywood hasn't been released as an official expansion *yet* (I'm looking at you, Mr. Jackson), but it's one that I've had a lot of real-world experience with over the past few years. Like all the other versions of *Munchkin* you or I have ever played, it's built around a simple dynamic: barge into a situation (possibly unprepared), stab your buddies, and steal their treasure. From there, it transmogrifies into the greatest, most constantly changing story you've ever told, complete with triumphs and setbacks, teamwork, treachery, wheeling and/or dealing, and ultimately the most fun you've had since that time you got drunk and limboed into the prevailing wind with your pants off.

(Or so I'm told.) In fact, the game is so much fun, the moment you wrap up one session, you can't wait to do it all again. (Television, that is, not the pantsless limbo.)

"A new version of *Munchkin*? How does it work? How do you play?" I pretend to hear you ask excitedly.

Well, let me tell you.

It all starts with you looking for a class card in your initial hand. There are a lot of them out there: Character Actor, Reality TV Star, Publicist, Baldwin – a veritable cornucopia of roles to fill. You scan your starting hand and, lo and behold, you find your class straight away: Actor. Great. You've heard about these guys. They're usually broke, so you might want to get ready to sell your starting loot for a level, just to get a leg up.

Now's as good a time as any to take a look around the densely packed table. The heavyset guy over there got Producer. He's already doing deals with his neighbors and shaking hands. Oh dear. That skinny woman in the power tie, looking shifty and sizing everyone up, could be an Agent, but, no, she turns out to be the Writer. Keep your eye on her. One of your best friends seems to have settled on Extra. You've never liked that role; it could be a long game for her. The Critic seems to have wound up in the hands of the chatty one over there, who doesn't seem to get out much and is really struggling to make friends. And that guy in the scarf, the one organizing his cards in the most dramatically satisfying way possible? He just flipped up the Director.

The game starts and everyone jockeys for initial position, equipping their characters and squirreling away cards they hope to call upon in time of dire need – which will come along soon enough. There are a few halfhearted fights, but nothing notable enough to make the trades.

Your turn finally rolls around. *Boom!* You kick down a door with misguided enthusiasm. The monster staring you in the face is a level 1 Audition. The card describes the gig as "featured extra in a forgettable telemovie." Bad Stuff: "Nothing. No one cares." How vaguely depressing. But it's sitting right there in front of you, trying to make you fear it, so you might as well get this over with.

Since you've sold all your stuff, you're level 2. "You're no match for me, Audition!" you proclaim in your head. Wait a minute. Did you say that out loud? Your friends smile politely. Yep, you did. How embarrassing. Well, no matter; you're ready for battle and nothing can foil your triumph. You're reaching for the level token when one of those smiling friends, the Producer, lays down a card: "Perfect Headshot." He steals your monster, takes your treasure, and claims your level. There's nothing you can do about it but congratulate him on a move well played. (That and silently add his name to the box in your head marked *Revenge!*)

The game rolls on. A whole lot of nothing happens. To you, at least. Everyone else seems to be having a ball. Your Director friend needs a couple of levels to beat a monster and get further ahead. (A Late-Night Dating Infomercial? You almost laugh, but manage to keep the pro face on when doing the deal.) In return for your help, he'll give you a card he can't use: "Acting Coach" +3 (Actors Only). That'll help you fight the more difficult things lurking behind the doors to come. And, hey, it's better than the big pile of nothing you have now, right? Sure, pal. Enjoy your level.

Boom! You kick down another door, this time with gusto (and pesto; in all the excitement, you dropped your corn chip). You and your new +3 Acting Coach sidekick are ready to roll! Then your heart sinks. There it is. The BIG one: Star-Making Audition, level 20. You're nowhere near ready for this. Nope.

You'll never beat it and take its treasure. Worse, the Bad Stuff that happens when you fail is pretty bad: "If you're higher than level 3, it destroys your career. Discard whole hand and lose two levels." Hold on, though. With your whopping two levels, that doesn't apply to you, does it? Let's see: "Level 3 and below, it stands there and mocks you mercilessly. Then it takes your footgear, for some reason." (Hollywood is weird like that. Isn't it meant to be "the shirt off your back"? Maybe that's *Munchkin Vegas*.)

It's hopeless. You brace for the worst – and then it happens. Your buddies around the table see your two measly levels. You pose no threat to any of them, so as a group they offer you something that, at that moment, is the greatest thing in the world: pity. They're all willing to chip in and help you. For a price, of course. (This is a game of *Munchkin*, after all.)

Of course, you recognize this act of generosity for what it really is: an easy opportunity to take advantage of a guy down on his luck and get some loot in the process. But a win's a win, right? You take a heaping spoonful of their pity, and you serve yourself up two new levels. Best of all, you only had to give away three of your five treasures. You came away with an "Armor-ni Suit" +1 (+4 if you're George Clooney) and a "Secluded Two-Bedroom HQ" +1 (+3 against Paparazzi). Haven't they played this game before? Suckers.

Your march to victory has started in earnest. The opening gambits are over, and the middle game is heating up for everyone. Pity may have given you a leg up, but you're in the big leagues now. A few more turns and you're neck and neck with the leaders. Friends are falling away, and even the few you have left are eyeing you with poorly concealed annoyance. It was inevitable that you'd end up burning them, like you just did when the Writer asked for your help against a Horribly Written Script. Hey, you needed all the cards in your hand for your next combat. Besides, she got out of trouble with her Wishing Ring of Great Acting, even without your help, right?

Unfortunately, those annoyed chickens come home to roost almost immediately.

Another door opens in front of you. Another monster: First Script, level 12. Not too shabby. You're sitting on a cool 15 (and you didn't even have to be George Clooney). Better yet, defeating this First Script will get you a level and a veritable buttload of treasure. You dare to hope for a moment that everyone will leave you alone to take out the threat. You check your cards again, trying not to draw attention to yourself. Don't look nervous. Just another turn going on. Nothing to see here. These certainly aren't the droids *you're* looking for. No, sir.

They're not going to buy it. Your pity play and the betrayals that followed are too fresh in their memories. Besides, you're strong now. A threat to win. The Writer is the first to pipe up: "Do we want to let him take this one?" But it's the Critic (what a jerk) who makes the ever-deadly observation: "The Actor will be really close to winning if he gets this." That makes the others pause and, like a single, vengeful organism, they pounce. "A Last Minute Script Change" is the first card to fall, followed by "With a Dialogue Coach" and a couple more for good measure. All of a sudden, you're not facing a simple First Script, but a Scary, Career Defining First Script With a Dialogue Coach and a Last Minute Script Change. It's, like, level 31 now.

That stinks. Better check the Bad Stuff.

"It ruins you. Lose your class, items, and dignity. Also lose your footgear, for some reason."

Go figure.

That's all right. Just run away. You can come back from this. It's not worth the risk. And you're ready to go, die in hand, when the Producer slowly reaches for his cards. You grimace. He lays down "The Contract." The text on this one is written in teeny-tiny small print and seems to go on forever, but you eventually get to it: "Play when any Actor enters combat. Prevents Actor from running away."

Well, that's just a pain, but like all Hollywood contracts there's a loophole: "Actor may discard all cards and still run away."

And an amendment to the loophole: "Actors who run away will never work in this town again. You might as well be dead." Guess you'd better win.

You'd ask for help, but everyone seems to be plotting against you. And smiling. Like it's a game or something. Jerks. Except your one buddy over there, the Extra. She still seems friendly, like the game's been hard on her and she just needs a hug. But her cards suck. Even if she wanted to, she can't help you.

You can dispose of your +3 Acting Coach to get a one-off bonus of +10. Damn, better do that. That puts you at 22. What else have we got here . . . ? You desperately deploy the Eccentric Director (+5 to side of your choice) you'd been saving for late in the game. And, oh dear, that

buddy of yours is the only one you can use the card "Steal Another Actor's Lines" on. This gives you another +5, but forces the victim to give up all his cards. You smile apologetically at the Extra as you play the card, but she receives the half-hearted apology with the dead eyes of a murderer. That doesn't bode well, but you'll have to cross that bridge when you come to it. The good news is you've got it! It cost almost your whole hand, and a longstanding allegiance with the Extra, but gosh darn it, you beat this script.

Wait, what did the Critic just put down? "Reshoot"? Oh, no! Combat voided. It's like it never happened, except all the cards everyone played are lost. No levels. No treasures. Just one more name for the Revenge! Box.

This is pretty typical of the combats that mark the transition of a *Munchkin* session from the second act to the finale. Throughout the game, *Munchkin*'s rules encourage everyone to work together in a web of ever-shifting alliances, sometimes struggling toward mutual victories, sometimes foiling another player's rush for glory. In the middle game, players can still convince themselves that they have a chance, that there's a yellow-brick path to victory if they just play their cards right. That all comes to a close around the time the first player hits level 7. After that, each turn takes on magnified significance. Botch a combat and you screw up your chance to win, or, even worse, you clear the path to victory for someone else.

The endgame frequently kicks off with someone springing a trap card on the leader. "TV Rerun" is a classic. It makes you fight the topmost monster in the discard pile. Unfortunately for the current leader, that card is "The Ever-Shrinking Budget." It's not just the healthy level – 13 – that's the problem, though. This particular monster ignores the Director's level in combat, and guess who's in the lead? Bad Stuff: "Trip on the bottom line. Go down two levels, and drop all your Big items." No help from anyone else is forthcoming and the Director fails at running away, so he kisses his levels and his +3 Megaphone of Authority goodbye. He's lucky to escape with his Puffy Pants intact.

Small skirmishes follow. Somewhere along the way, your erstwhile ally the Extra plays "Steal the Scene, Go Up a Level," positioning herself to make a run for the lead, but you bring her down a notch with a sneaky "Writer Cuts Your Dialogue" trap. (Again? You really are a bad person, you know.) You can declare that alliance dead and buried. Ah, well.

Finally it's the Producer's turn. At level 9, he's hoping that at least some of those earlier handshake-sealed deals will pay off. The table holds its breath. The people do, too. The Producer kicks down the door.

Lurking there is a seemingly harmless action card, "Press Embargo." It lets you stop one player from using cards or abilities for two turns. Everyone breathes a sigh of relief and waits for the Producer to loot the room and move on. He doesn't, though. He looks for trouble – in this case a level 18 Studio Executive drawn from his hand. (The John

Kovalic art for this one is a smile holding a machine gun. I think I know the model.) There's no running from this guy. He comes in smiling and fires everyone in his field of vision. Bad Stuff: "Everybody's fired. You're dead and go down two levels, unless –" everyone perks up at this "– you play a card to help the Studio Executive to win the combat."

The sweet smell of self-preservation hangs in the air. The Producer shifts uneasily in his seat, trying to look confident. He knew there would be risks, but you have to play the cards you have when the opportunity to win arises. The Critic clears her throat, which suggests she must have a doozy of a punishment to dole out on this one. Everyone else seems a bit more unsure of themselves.

But the Producer's no fool. He's prepared for the war. He's level 9. Add +2 thanks to "Nifty Track Record of Success." That brings him to 11. Next comes "Expensive Shiny Suit of  Blinding," +4. "Far Too Fancy and Intimidating Luxury SUV" gives him a helpful +6. "Friend in Production" and "Sterling Silver Tongue" both send +5 his way. When all his cards are played and bonuses tallied, he's sitting on 36. This fight isn't going to be pretty.

Nervous players eye their fellow munchkins with scarcely suppressed suspicion. Nobody wants to burn all their best cards, but if they hesitate, they risk the Producer running over them as he storms to victory. (Did you see how fancy and intimidating his SUV is?) Besides, only total idiots oppose Studio Executives.

One by one, players throw in a card. The Director and the Critic race each other for the chance to help first. Both offer big-point cards. From the Director it's "Evil" (+5 to Monster), and from the Critic it's "With a Reputation" (also +5). So The Producer is now staring at an Evil Studio Executive With a Reputation, level 28. Not good enough.

The Writer throws in a Wandering Monster. Adding a Star With a Bloated Contract to the Executive's posse is a nice touch, but it's only level 6. That gets the opposition up to 34. We're still short.

All eyes turn to you, and you shrug noncommittally. The Extra mutters something guaranteed to get the MPAA to slap the conversation with an R. Then she grumbles "Difficult Actor" – the card, not the person, though she is glaring in your direction as she says it. That will be another +5 for the Studio Executive.

Before the card leaves the Extra's hand, though, the Producer slaps her with that "Press Embargo" he'd just acquired. Guess it wasn't so harmless after all. Locked out of the action, the Extra can only scowl and, like extras everywhere, wait for the featured players to get their acts together.

The Producer leans back in his chair, takes a fistful of potato chips, and stuffs them in his mouth, savoring the taste. The other munchkins wilt under his triumphant gaze. He lets out a hearty laugh.

That's when you strike, with a card you've been holding since the start of the game: "Plot Device." (See what I did there?) It puts the target's combat strength at one point more than its opponent's, no matter how far behind it is, so the Studio Executive is now at 37. You and the Writer share knowing looks. It's her favorite card, after all. Just in case the Producer holds anything else useful in his depleted hand, the Writer throws "Executive Producer" and shouts "That's a wrap!" No one else can play a card, so the battle is over.

The Studio Executive does his damage. The Producer is dead, and the Extra along with him. You try to argue that the Extra technically tried to help out in combat (hey, you owed it to her for old time's sake), but the majority vote her to Extra Valhalla. The Critic can barely contain her glee as she takes the first grab at your loot. Otherwise it's high-fives among the other survivors and a massive sigh of relief at the disaster you banded together to avert.

No one has quite recovered from the Studio Executive Massacre by the time your turn rolls around again. You couldn't have planned it any better.

You're at level 8, so you sell everything except for your Artistic Integrity. (That gives you +3.) It all adds up to a level, so you're suddenly on the threshold of victory.

Your fellow munchkins are nervous. Just look at that Director sweat. Ah, life is sweet. But you can't get too cocky. A glance down at the cards you have left reminds you that you're looking pretty naked, but that's the price you sometimes pay to be an Actor. (At least that's what you tell yourself to get to sleep at night.)

With your Artistic Integrity clutched in a strategic location, you kick down what you hope will be the last door of the game. You also pray to whoever's listening that you're not going to come up against a level 20 Rehab Clinic or something equally challenging. (If you were a Reality TV Star, you'd love to turn up Rehab Clinic. You get levels from that battle whether you win or lose.) No, you want something simple, something you can stomp with ease.

You dramatically flip the card, revealing . . . Dual Threat, the *Munchkin Hollywood* equivalent of Super Munchkin.

That "Philanthropist" class card you've had hanging around in your hand for a while now comes into play because, why not? The Critic makes a comment about irony, but no one is listening.

Operation Win (it's a technical term) continues. You don't loot the room. That would be madness. Instead, you look for trouble and put down the only opponent from your own hand. Your final monster: "Heartbreaking Death Scene."

The Death Scene is level 12, but it might as well be level 100 for all the resources you have. (Okay, no; 100 would still be much worse.) That earlier fire sale suddenly looks a little less brilliant. You're level 9, plus the bonus for your Artistic Integrity makes you 12. A tie. Typical.

The Bad Stuff doesn't matter, because if you mess this up, you're done. It's back to the minor leagues and winning – well, winning will be what other people do.

You pause and wait for your fellow munchkins to toss in a few cards and bury you, but no one has a thing. The Press Embargo is still muting the Extra, and the Studio Executive battle has left everyone else pretty much toothless. Frantically you review the two cards left in your hand, as if reading them again will transform them into something useful. No such luck. They remain a curse card, "Lose Your Class," and "Harsh Spotlight," which makes the monster even more difficult to defeat.

Nothing. You're still tied.

Maybe Operation Win wasn't quite as smart as it first seemed, but at least you're playing to type. Actors aren't especially famous for their incredible long-term planning. They have other strengths – resiliency, blind hope, an ability to read and memorize words – but great foresight is not one of them.

Wait a minute: Learning words. That's totally your thing. And you definitely read something important on your Class card. Read it again, you fool! "Actors win ties in combat against Scenes."

You announce to the table that, against all odds, you are actually in a state of Win.

"I thought of the Actor's ability to win on a tie, like, five minutes ago," the Critic sneers.

For the first time ever, you're grateful to the Critic. She's drawing a lot of the annoyance that might otherwise be directed your way right now.

Still, no one deploys a card. Trying to mask your growing excitement, you tentatively ask, "So . . . um . . . does that mean . . . I . . . ?"

The Producer leans across the table, his hand extended. "Well done. It looks like you won the game."

You breathe again. Everyone else breathes again. The table breathes again. People start munching on snacks and the room buzzes with cheerful conversation. Sure, some are a little disappointed at losing, but there's a lot more to the game than that.

You've all been through a hell of a ride and told one hell of a story together. I mean, who won't remember when the Extra took on the Postmodern Theatre Re-Enactment of a Miscast Big-Budget Comedy (consensus in the room made it Arnold Schwarzenegger's *Junior*) armed with nothing but an Extra-Large Sense of Self-Importance, a Pillow, and some well-timed Olive Oil, only for the Writer to steal the victory at the last minute with a Renegotiated Contract? Of course the Writer got her comeuppance when she kicked down a door concealing an Eighties Child Star, only to have the nightmare compounded by the Critic, who added a truly awful Wandering Monster to the mix: a Paparazzo with a Telephoto Lens and Friends in the Tabloid Press. The Extra tried to save the day, to no avail. But, hey, she went down swinging at that Paparazzo with her Photo-Hating Radioactive Dog-in-a-Handbag.

By the time the dust settles and the cards are being gathered up and shuffled, you're all buddies once more. Better friends than ever, in fact, and you can't wait to start up a new story together.

As a great man once said: All the world's a stage, and all the men and women merely munchkins."

Now if you'll excuse me, I have a buddy whose treasure needs stealing. . . . ✴

Liam McIntyre is a giant nerd. He's not shy about it. He spent too much of his life playing video games, collecting miniatures, and trying to invent new board games. This made him a real hit with the ladies. At some stage he decided he wanted to be an actor. Then, years later, he was surprised to discover that, all evidence to the contrary, he was, in fact, Spartacus. He's also been known to menace the Flash in the guise of the Weather Wizard. Liam resides in Los Angeles, c/o The New World, with his beautiful wife, Erin, and a really great character in *Skyrim*. When he returns home to Terra Australis, he reconnects with his friends through the age-old art of *Munchkin*. It's amazing they're still friends, really. They're pretty cool, too, in case you were wondering.

DUCK DUCK BOOM

Draw a duck on something. Pass this duck around the table, starting with the player on your left. Each player must roll a d6. On a 1-5, nothing happens. On a 6, the duck explodes. If it explodes on you, it showers you with treasure. Draw three Treasure cards. If it explodes on another player, it showers them with Death.

My Favorite Munchkin

John Kovalic

Backstabbing buddies and ducks found in dungeons,
Alluring ol' kneepads and monsters you bludgeon.
Lined end to end they will go on for yards,
These are a few of my favorite cards.

W hat's your favorite *Munchkin* card?"
It's a question I get asked. A lot.

The quick answer – kind of a cop-out, really – is that I don't have a favorite. I've now drawn more than 5,000 cards for the *Munchkin* game series. You try picking *your* most beloved out of 5,000 of your kids, you monster!

But that's not entirely true.

In the 15 years I've been privileged to be part of the *Munchkin* team, there are certain cards that I just feel happier about than others, once they're drawn. The reasons can be anything – perhaps it's a sly glance a monster seems to make, once it's inked; a hidden reference to some other card, maybe; a graphic in-joke; or simply any card with a toilet on it.

I'm given a lot of leeway with *Munchkin* cards, once the art specs arrive from either Steve Jackson or Andrew Hackard. Both pretty much know what to expect from me. If I get a card spec along the lines of "A munchkin wrapped head-to-toe in toilet paper, maybe with the rest of the roll on the ground nearby" (*yes*, this happened – *find it!*), it's safe to say we all can imagine what the finished art is going to look at least a little like.

Sometimes – and I am not making this up – the art spec is simply "You know what to do, John." The simple fact remains: Yes. Yes, I *do* know what to do. This scares me.

Often, my favorites come from the most recent set I've drawn. I like to think I'm a better artist now than I was 10 or 12 years ago. At the very least, I'm *happier* with my work these days. I believe that the line quality is tighter, the composition better, and the characters more animated.

I consciously try and make each set better than the last, and the art is constantly evolving. It's part of what keeps drawing *Munchkin* fresh and fun for me. Given that the most recent cards are, at the moment, the most interesting, coming up with an unskewed list of my 10 favorite *Munchkin* cards would be problematic. I know. I try. Often.

But choosing my favorites from each set? That's easier. There are cards that stand out for me in every batch. I can be notoriously hard on my early work. Still, there are certainly some pieces I remember fondly, the ones that came out juuuuuuust right. So here, at last, are all the *Munchkin* core sets I've drawn. And from each one, I've chosen a few of my favorite cards.

This is the first time I've ever had to sit down and look back over every card I've ever drawn for *Munchkin*. It's an odd feeling, reviewing everything like that, even more so when it's in the name of talking about my own "best" work. In my defense, this is the essay my editor requested of me. Really. Even so, it's taken some effort for me to rule out my usual "Here's my artwork . . . it's not too awful, I guess" approach to these kinds of questions.

So while modesty dictates I should flee screaming at this point (+1 to Run Away), I'll instead roll up my sleeves and kick down that door. . . .

MUNCHKIN (2001)

FUN FACT: I vividly remember when Steve Jackson Games sent me my contributor copies of Munchkin, *mostly because my first thought was, "Nobody in their right mind is going to pay $25 for just a bunch of cards and a single die." That was 29 printings ago.*

I recall the original *Munchkin* set being a bit rushed. I think I was working on another project for Steve at the time – possibly *Chez Geek*-related – and I needed to finish *Munchkin* off quicker than I would have liked. I was utterly thrilled to be the artist on a game that Steve himself designed, though, so I wasn't even thinking about turning the project down. I adored the game and loved the unapologetic silliness of it all – even if I believed a light, humorous fantasy card game would be a niche-market product, at best. The cards were hilarious, the game was a hoot, and that was all that mattered.

Despite being hurried, the art – I think – worked. There's a sense of manic energy that the deadline pressure may have brought to these cards, something I've tried to recapture in each subsequent release (the energy, that is – not the deadline pressure). People seem to love the drawings in this set, and some of the cards ("Gazebo," "Chicken on Your Head," "Kneepads of Allure") have become iconic. Part of me would love to redraw this entire set some day. The fear of being pelted with dice and detritus by outraged fans of the game holds me back from lobbying too hard for this.

That said, "Duck of Doom" is my favorite here; it helped define the silliness that would run through all *Munchkin*, but it's also evil. "Duck of Doom" is certainly a card I'd still be happy to have drawn in any subsequent set, and it's become one of *Munchkin*'s truly unforgettable images.

STAR MUNCHKIN (2002)

FUN FACT: There are no blank cards in any Munchkin core sets. This has saved my drawing arm at more conventions than I care to count.

As a cartoonist, it's no fun revisiting your work from years ago. Heck, sometimes I hate revisiting my work from a few months ago. But I'm not gonna lie — I'm surprised at how well *Star Munchkin* has aged. Going over the cards again, I see the embryonic beginnings of a definite *Munchkin* style; I was gaining confidence, and I had a bit more time to finish this set. I remember "Sidekick: Loud Hairy Alien" being as fun to draw as it still looks, to me; the "Cyborgs" and "Space Goats" turned out nicely; and one of the promo cards, "Heart of the Anomaly," has gone on to become the single most sought-after *Munchkin* card in existence. One sold for more than $1,000 on eBay.

This is a tough one. "Being of Impure Thought"? "Duct Tape"?

In the end, the *Doctor Who* fan in me still loves "Dogbot" most of all. Possibly for no other reason than it's "Dogbot."

MUNCHKIN BITES (2004)

FUN FACT: At a convention in Minneapolis, I met Marv Wolfman and found out he was a Munchkin fan. So we added Marv the Wolfman to this set in his honor.

The art deadlines for both *Munchkin Fu* and *Munchkin Bites* were relatively close together; there was also a *Chez Geek* project in the works. (At the time, *Chez Geek* was still the larger franchise.) We were all worried about my ability to do three major releases in such a short period of time, and I suggested that the immensely talented Greg Hyland be given *Munchkin Fu*, which turned out wonderfully.

I drew most of *Munchkin Bites* during the summer of 2003, sitting outside various pubs on the banks of the Thames, in Southwark, London. It was glorious. I can recommend no better venue for drawing *Munchkin* cards. Also, I may have become slightly addicted to Pimm's because of this. That definitely helped when I was designing the werewolves and changelings.

"Stake-A-Matic" and "Wind-Up Skull" are both cards that still make me giggle, but "Vampire Hunter" (based on my pal Sonia) is my favorite. It's got a little more detail than most *Munchkin* cards did back then and is nicely energetic.

SUPER MUNCHKIN (2005)

FUN FACT: I drew the first Munchkin *sets with Ultra Fine Point Sharpies. I am not proud of this, but at the time, it was what I was using for all my work. They are cheap and easy to use, but the line quality stinks. I didn't know any better. Wait! This isn't a Fun Fact at all! It's just sad. . . .*

Super Munchkin was the fourth *Munchkin* core set I worked on? Really? I always remembered it as being one of the first. Never trust a cartoonist's judgment. Lesson learned.

Looking back over *Super Munchkin* is a bit of a revelation; this is one of those sets I don't play as often as others. My drawings seem to again be gaining confidence, and – huh, look at that – there's an energy to these that wasn't there in the earlier sets. I was using horrible pens, yes, but I enjoyed drawing this set enormously. There's far more action here than there was in *Munchkin Bites*. "Molybdenum Skateboard" and "Flight" are both evocative of the fun I was having, but "Touched Ancient Idol" is my stone-cold favorite of the set. Why would you touch an ancient idol? *Why would you touch an ancient idol?* I believe I captured a certain essential stupidity nicely on this one. Capturing stupidity is important when drawing *Munchkin*.

MUNCHKIN IMPOSSIBLE (2006)

FUN FACT: Munchkin Impossible *is the only core* Munchkin *set I've drawn that does not yet have a supplement. It's a great set, but* Munchkin Cthulhu *was released soon after, and was a huge hit.* Munchkin Impossible *was caught in the explosion of a gaming supernova. We still hope to get back to it some day, though. There aren't enough tuxedos in* Munchkin. *Or martinis.*

Confession time: In all honesty, there are some stylistic aspects of the early- to mid-period *Munchkin* drawings I wish I'd never, ever glommed on to. Specifically, the Stupefying Tremendous Overbite. The Stupefying Tremendous Overbite is something I'd draw on the characters when I'd want to show them grinning, but manic. I used it in my comic book, *Dork Tower*. It was a stylistic quirk I picked up from cartoonist Carol Lay. (Her *Story Minute* and *Way Lay* strips were simply fantastic.) But I took it to unfeasible extremes. I believe it reached its zenith with *Munchkin Impossible*; the main character appears frequently, smirking with a disturbing James Bond-meets-*Hee Haw* zealotry.

That said, going through all the cards again, I'm probably happier with this set than the Stupefying Tremendous Overbite problem might otherwise deserve. The "Seduce Enemy Agent" duo, "Shoe Blades," "Cheat Death," and "Deep Cover Assignment" all make me happy. But my favorite? "Learn From Experience."

And I did indeed learn from experience: I banished the overbite from my drawings.

MUNCHKIN CTHULHU (2007)

FUN FACT: The "Cultist" card, showing the titular character holding a statue, is a tip of the pen to an Illuminati: New World Order *card I did for Steve Jackson back in the 1990s.* Illuminati *was my first professional gaming gig. Try and spot my cards in it: I did 20 of them!*

Munchkin Cthulhu was the turning point. Look, I loved working on all the *Munchkin* sets prior to this one. But by 2007, it was obvious that the game was becoming something special. *Very* special. Those who know me also know I'm a Cthulhu freak, as is Steve. In a sense, *Munchkin Cthulhu* could just as easily have been called *Munchkin No-Brainer*. We were prepared to lose Sanity points with this one.

Coming hot on the heels of *Munchkin Impossible*, *Cthulhu* let me switch from drawing contemporary characters to historical ones. For a very silly card game, I still wanted to get the clothing styles *correct*. This is where good reference materials come in, and *The Chronicles of Western Fashion*, by John Peacock, was a huge boon to the look of the game.

I had scads of time to complete this set, and I loved every minute of it. "Chibithulhu" went on to spawn its own mini-franchise. I'm also happy with the quasi-caricatures of "Aughost Derwraith" and "H. P. Munchcraft." But it's the simple little "Elder Globs" – playing off of soft drink characters from my youth – that remains my favorite.

THE GOOD, THE BAD, AND THE MUNCHKIN (2007)

FUN FACT: Some artists hate drawing feet. Me? I hated drawing horses. I had never come up with a good horse drawing that fit my style of cartooning. The Good, The Bad, and the Munchkin meant that I suddenly had to draw many, many horses. Because of this, I'm now much better at drawing horses. Go up a level!

The massive success of *Munchkin Cthulhu* shouldn't have come as such a surprise to anyone. But by the time the art specs for *The Good, The Bad, and the Munchkin* came in, there was a very palpable sense among those of us working on it that the line was only getting bigger and better.

My cartooning career began with me drawing funny animals – specifically, a muskrat named Carson, in my comic strips *Wild Life*, and later, *Dork Tower*. So I really enjoyed all the animal cards in this set: "Catamount," "Coyote," "Grizzly Bear." Even "Exterminate a Bison

Herd" is sort of animal-based, in an awful, awful way. But there's something about the expression on the doomed protagonist's face on "Shoot the Piano Player" that keeps it my favorite.

By the way, I now want to do a game called *Catamount, Coyote, Grizzly Bear*. Or possibly that's the name of my new indie band.

MUNCHKIN BOOTY (2008)

FUN FACT: In every Munchkin *set, one monster becomes the Loser: the hapless, put-upon protagonist of almost every card that features something foul and unnatural happening to a creature. The Net Troll created this position in classic* Munchkin *(and has become one of the game's best-loved monsters because of it). For* Munchkin Booty, *it seemed fittingly ridiculous to let the Clam take this spotlight.*

I group *Munchkin Cthulhu, The Good, The Bad, and the Munchkin,* and *Munchkin Booty* together as sort of a transitional period for my cartooning. They were the three releases that defined in my mind what *Munchkin* should look like going forward. Possibly it was the quasi-historical research the character designs now required, making me think more about little details that went into them. Possibly it was the growing sales numbers, and the "Holy *carp*, these drawings had better be good!" mentality that came along with it. But in the Beatles discography of *Munchkin* games, these are, to me, the *Help!, Rubber Soul,* and *Revolver* of the catalogue. Though Weird Al might be a better musical metaphor for a game like *Munchkin*.

"Sir Francis Drake" could have been my favorite here, but it was squished into a teeny tiny little space, because of all the card text. "Almighty Cod" makes me grin, but "Cutlass" is my favorite, again loosely based on my pal Sonia. Wait. What? Is Sonia my *Munchkin* muse? At the very least, she's really fun to draw!

MUNCHKIN ZOMBIES (2010)

FUN FACT: *My daughter was born in 2008. This was the first* Munchkin *set I drew as a daddy, and I asked – politely – if someone else could draw the "Meals on Wheels" card. I just couldn't bring myself to draw zombies going after a baby in a pram at that point in time.*

Following what I remember as back-to-back-to-back big *Munchkin* releases, there was a two-year break between *Munchkin Booty* and *Munchkin Zombies*. It was welcome, and let me recharge my batteries, at least a bit.

Don't get me wrong – there were plenty of other *Munchkin* projects to get done. There always are: supplements, promo cards, plushies, T-shirts. They all hit fast and furious. *Munchkin* had become a sales behemoth by 2010. But I went into *Zombies* excited by the prospect of designing new characters for a new set for the first time in a couple of years.

There had been zombies in *Munchkin* before, sure, but *Zombies* gave me a chance to redesign them from the ground (the underground?) up. This made it an exciting, dynamic project, and I was psyched about it. Nobody asked, but if there were a "Most Fun *Munchkin* Projects to Have Worked On" list, this would be in the top three.

Personal highlights here included animating the shambling zombie corpses on cards such as "Roller Skate," seeing how much extra blood-splatter I could add to the butcher as a "Wandering Monster," and tossing my great pal Kenneth Hite in as the "Zombieologist." Simple cards such as "Mailbox" and "Perfect Hiding Place" delight me to this day. My favorite card, however, must be "Brains Enough for Two." Sick, twisted, and cute. When I was penciling it, I tweeted that the card art was "the most gruesome thing *Munchkin* has ever made me draw."

As Andrew Hackard has designed more and more cards, I've had to tweet that same line several times since.

MUNCHKIN CONAN (2012)

FUN FACT: Snake-beasts. Why did it have to be snake-beasts? There were a lot of them in this set. If I never have to sketch another frog-god or snake-beast again as long as I live, I will be a happy, happy man.

This was the first, big licensed *Munchkin* game I drew. (Obviously Steve Jackson Games wasn't going to do something silly like have me redesign *Axe Cop* or anything.) Heck, it's the first big-deal licensed *anything* I've been involved with.

Working on an official Robert E. Howard *Munchkin* set was thrilling.

Creating a cartoonish Conan was a dream come true.

It also scared the hell out of me.

So many legendary artists had already put their marks on the world and people of Cimmeria and beyond. Dank places where evil dwelled? Sorcerers of dour and mysterious intent? A few extra tentacles thrown in for good measure? Thoth-Amon and/or Nabonidus the Red Priest and/or various shambling masses? Check! All there, and all done by the greats. I mean, seriously: I was using Frank Frazetta and Bernie Wrightson as reference sources. "Intimidating" doesn't even begin to cover it!

None of them had ever drawn Ducks of Doom, though, so I got over it.

I enjoyed coming up with a comic Conan that worked in the *Munchkin* universe, yet remained respectful of Howard's creation. Well, as respectful as a three-fingered doodle with wildly violent tendencies could be. It's fitting that my favorite card in the set is the one that encompasses the spirit of Conan perfectly: "What Is Best in Life?"

That it is also one of the very few cards in *Munchkin* that lets you go up two levels makes it that much sweeter.

MUNCHKIN APOCALYPSE (2012)

FUN FACT: Did you know the Scientists in Apocalypse *are all based on the Atomic Zombies from* Munchkin Zombies? *They are doomed!* Doomed!

There was much for me to love in *Munchkin Apocalypse*, and pound for pound, it may be my favorite set, art-wise, overall. It was outrageously entertaining to work on, even though it had to be completed in record time. You know, to make sure it was released before the 2012 Mayan apocalypse.

Steve, Andrew, and Phil flew up to Madison, and we discussed the cards, throwing ideas back and forth. What's not to love about a kid whacking a monstrous gourd with a first aid kit? Some old favorites returned, with sharks (first seen in *Booty*) and zombies making cameo appearances. Plus, I got to draw musicians Molly Lewis and the Doubleclicks for the special *Munchkin Apocalypse* promotional bookmark, "The Ladies of Ragnarok."

It's embarrassingly difficult to choose a personal favorite from this set, but if you put a triple-barreled slingshot to my head, I believe the mindlessly happy, shimmying couple in "Safety Dance" best reflects how I felt working on *Munchkin Apocalypse*.

MUNCHKIN PATHFINDER (2013)

FUN FACT: Paizo, publishers of the Pathfinder *roleplaying game, sent me a massive box of* Pathfinder *goodies as reference materials. When the box arrived, it was like Christmas morning. Things like this often lead me to believe I have made the right Life Choices.*

Two of the last four *Munchkin* core sets I've drawn have been licensed products. On a certain gamer geek level, I think I was even more thrilled to play in Paizo's *Pathfinder* sandbox than I was in Conan's. I'm a roleplaying gamer at heart, and I have always cherished the *Pathfinder* RPG. Being able to dive deep into its lush, detailed background was my own personal spell of Righteous Might. The good folks at Paizo were wonderful to work with, and *Munchkin* czar Andrew Hackard came up with a superb card list.

Andrew likes to say that he can tell by my artwork when I'm really charged up about a project, and this was definitely one of those times. Can we talk about the Red Mantis Assassins for a second? Anything to do with the Red Mantis Assassins. Man, I loved drawing those guys. What's not to love about overly serious characters running around wearing goofy bug helmets? Especially the one that needed to lose a few pounds.

One of the earliest cards I drew remains my favorite: "Hobbes Goblin." Being able to work a Bill Watterson tribute into a *Munchkin* game was like the icing on a cake that was already buried under a ton of icing in the first place!

MUNCHKIN LEGENDS (2013)

FUN FACT: Munchkin Legends *was the last* Munchkin *set I drew at my downtown studio in Madison. It was a terrific studio, right above a bar called the Tipsy Cow. But downtown Madison was fast becoming a distraction . . . as was trying to pry their share of the rent out of my studio mates. So I moved to a studio in the country, on my own. It may not be as prestigious as being on Madison's Capitol Square, but it's been enormously beneficial to both my productivity* and *my blood pressure.*

I'm an ancient history nut, so *Munchkin Legends* was a particularly apt set for me to sink my teeth into. It was also a very hush-hush one, as are most *Munchkin* new releases now. This meant that I couldn't say anything about it publicly while I was drawing the cards – which is probably okay, as I'd only have kept tweeting "ZOMG I LOVE THIS SET!" over and over again, until I'd lost every Twitter follower I ever had.

Yes, this *was* a particularly rewarding set for me. As such, it may also be the most difficult one of them all from which to choose a favorite. "Passion Potion" and "Viking Duck" are visual riffs off of classic *Munchkin*'s "Kneepads of Allure" and "Duck of Doom." "Sewer Gator" and "Loch Ness Monster" also make me giggle. But in the end, I have to give the nod to "Kraken" and "Flying Monkeys" – two

cards that work for me because of the expressions on the monsters' faces: one mighty (and hungry), the other resigned and, frankly, doomed.

MUNCHKIN OZ (2015)

FUN FACT: I was visiting my family in London when I got the call that we needed a cover for an emergency secret Munchkin *Project as soon as possible. I always travel with pens (Faber-Castell PITT artist pens, fine and superfine nibs), pencils (Palomino 602s), and paper (four-ply Bristol Board). "Emergency cartooning" is a thing that happens more often than you might think, where* Munchkin *is concerned. . . .*

Munchkin Oz was by far the tightest deadline I have ever been given for a major project. Seriously. If I told you what it was, you'd never believe me. Possibly it was the sheer adrenaline-fueled panic that added a certain spark to the work, but in the end, sore wrist and all, I felt this turned out to be one of the prettiest *Munchkin* sets we've ever produced.

The illustrations from the original L. Frank Baum Oz books (by both W. W. Denslow and then, from the second book on, John R. Neill) were wonderful. However, they felt, to me, very Victorian: lovely, classic, but dated – not a look I felt was right for *Munchkin*. I became a huge fan of Skottie Young's work for the multi-Eisner Award-winning Marvel Comics Oz graphic novels, and the energy and vibrancy that leapt off their pages became my inspiration for *Munchkin Oz*. I had huge fun with classic characters such as the Sawhorse, H. M. Woggle-Bug, and Jack Pumpkinhead. But lord help me if one of Andrew's silliest cards, "This Is Not the Oz You're Looking For," didn't become my favorite.

Doomed adventurers and undone monsters are common themes in *Munchkin*, but the game itself, thankfully, has proved to be anything but. What are the expansions I'm working on right now? I can't tell you, but they are *so cool*. Playing in Steve Jackson's Atomic Toybox is a ridiculously rewarding experience, and as long as I'm here, I hope to keep *Munchkin* looking better and better . . . and its adventurers more doomed.

Gotta go now – I've got some cards to draw. And I've a hunch one or two of them may turn out to be my new favorites! ✴

Munchkin illustrator **John Kovalic**'s cartoons have appeared everywhere from *The New York Times* to *Dragon* magazine to games that have sold in the millions. His comic creations include the critically acclaimed comic strips and comic books *Dork Tower* and *Dr. Blink: Superhero Shrink*. A co-founder and co-owner of Out of the Box Games, and a cartoonist for Steve Jackson Games, John has illustrated over 100 games and game supplements, including *Apples to Apples*, *INWO*, and *Chez Geek*. He was the first cartoonist inducted into the Academy of Adventure Gaming Arts and Design Hall of Fame in 2004. His game design credits include *ROFL!* and *Double Feature*. Kovalic has drawn more than 5,000 cards for *Munchkin* and wouldn't mind a spot of whiskey because of it. In his spare time, he searches for spare time.